"If you are ready to be refreshed as well as challenged, read this book. It is biblical and practical. Its clarity is powerful and very compelling. Thank you, Mark Dever and Jamie Dunlop, for loving the church of Jesus Christ!"

Ronnie Floyd, President, the Southern Baptist Convention; Senior Pastor, Cross Church, Springdale, Arkansas

"*The Compelling Community* could not have come at a better time. Its arguments are compelling. What we need today are not new methods for church growth, but a fresh yielding to the Holy Spirit so that he can take us back to the gospel-centered principles we see in the New Testament that catapulted the early church into the center stage of human history. Thank you, Mark and Jamie, for refreshing our spirits with these timeless truths."

Conrad Mbewe, Pastor, Kabwata Baptist Church, Lusaka, Zambia

"*The Compelling Community* provides an alternative to running your church on the building blocks of specialization and segmentation. The book is well-timed. After all, many of us long to see the gospel build community along the lines of generalization and integration instead. Great stuff from two men who have given their lives to the welfare of the local church."

David R. Helm, Pastor, Holy Trinity Church, Chicago; Chairman, The Charles Simeon Trust

"Many of us live in neighborhoods with an abundance of church congregations, yet those neighborhoods are flooded with crime, racism, lostness, and very few changed lives. Have you ever wondered why churches are not having more of an impact? This powerful and convicting book should challenge every church to do a self-examination to determine if their weekly gatherings are making an impact in their community through the power of the gospel!"

Fred Luter Jr., Pastor, Franklin Avenue Baptist Church, New Orleans, Louisiana

"Mark Dever and Jamie Dunlop remind us that the faithful local church is ever seeking to make a compelling case for Christ in community."

Tony Carter, Pastor, East Point Church, East Point, Georgia

THE
COMPELLING
COMMUNITY

Other 9Marks Books

The Pastor and Counseling: The Basics of Shepherding Members in Need, Jeremy Pierre and Deepak Reju (2015)

Who Is Jesus?, Greg Gilbert (2015)

Nine Marks of a Healthy Church, 3rd edition, Mark Dever (2013)

Finding Faithful Elders and Deacons, Thabiti M. Anyabwile (2012)

Am I Really a Christian?, Mike McKinley (2011)

What Is the Gospel?, Greg Gilbert (2010)

Biblical Theology in the Life of the Church: A Guide for Ministry, Michael Lawrence (2010)

Church Planting Is for Wimps: How God Uses Messed-up People to Plant Ordinary Churches That Do Extraordinary Things, Mike McKinley (2010)

It Is Well: Expositions on Substitutionary Atonement, Mark Dever and Michael Lawrence (2010)

What Does God Want of Us Anyway? A Quick Overview of the Whole Bible, Mark Dever (2010)

The Church and the Surprising Offense of God's Love: Reintroducing the Doctrines of Church Membership and Discipline, Jonathan Leeman (2010)

What Is a Healthy Church Member?, Thabiti M. Anyabwile (2008)

12 Challenges Churches Face, Mark Dever (2008)

The Gospel and Personal Evangelism, Mark Dever (2007)

What Is a Healthy Church?, Mark Dever (2007)

Building Healthy Churches

Edited by Mark Dever and Jonathan Leeman

Church Elders: How to Shepherd God's People Like Jesus, Jeramie Rinne (2014)

Evangelism: How the Whole Church Speaks of Jesus, J. Mack Stiles (2014)

Expositional Preaching: How We Speak God's Word Today, David R. Helm (2014)

The Gospel: How the Church Portrays the Beauty of Christ, Ray Ortlund (2014)

Sound Doctrine: How a Church Grows in the Love and Holiness of God, Bobby Jamieson (2013)

Church Discipline: How the Church Protects the Name of Jesus, Jonathan Leeman (2012)

Church Membership: How the World Knows Who Represents Jesus, Jonathan Leeman (2012)

THE COMPELLING COMMUNITY

*Where God's Power Makes
a Church Attractive*

MARK DEVER &
JAMIE DUNLOP

CROSSWAY

WHEATON, ILLINOIS

The Compelling Community: Where God's Power Makes a Church Attractive

Copyright © 2015 by Mark Dever and Jamie Dunlop

Published by Crossway
    1300 Crescent Street
    Wheaton, Illinois 60187

Cover design: Mark Davis

Cover image: Sideways Design/Shutterstock.com

First printing 2015

Printed in the United States of America

Trade paperback ISBN: 978-1-4335-4354-8
ePub ISBN: 978-1-4335-4357-9
PDF ISBN: 978-1-4335-4355-5
Mobipocket ISBN: 978-1-4335-4356-2

Library of Congress Cataloging-in-Publication Data
Dever, Mark.
    The compelling community : where God's power makes
a church attractive / Mark Dever and Jamie Dunlop.
        pages cm. — (9Marks books)
    Includes bibliographical references and index.
        1. Church. 2. Communities—Religious aspects—
Christianity. I. Title.
BV600.3.D48   2015
253—dc23   2014028681

Crossway is a publishing ministry of Good News Publishers.

VP		25	24	23	22	21	20	19	18	17	16	15
15	14	13	12	11	10	9	8	7	6	5	4	3	2

To our church, with joy and gratitude

"For what thanksgiving can
we return to God for you,
for all the joy that we feel for
your sake before our God?"

Contents

Series Preface

The 9Marks series of books is premised on two basic ideas. First, the local church is far more important to the Christian life than many Christians today perhaps realize. We at 9Marks believe that a healthy Christian is a healthy church member.

Second, local churches grow in life and vitality as they organize their lives around God's Word. God speaks. Churches should listen and follow. It's that simple. When a church listens and follows, it begins to look like the One it is following. It reflects his love and holiness. It displays his glory. A church will look like him as it listens to him. By this token, the reader might notice that all "9 marks," taken from Mark Dever's book, *Nine Marks of a Healthy Church* (Crossway, 3rd ed., 2013), begin with the Bible:

- expositional preaching;
- biblical theology;
- a biblical understanding of the gospel;
- a biblical understanding of conversion;
- a biblical understanding of evangelism;
- a biblical understanding of church membership;
- a biblical understanding of church discipline;
- a biblical understanding of discipleship and growth; and
- a biblical understanding of church leadership.

More can be said about what churches should do in order to be healthy, such as pray. But these nine practices are the ones that we believe are most often overlooked today (unlike prayer). So our basic message to churches is, don't look to the best business practices or the latest styles; look to God. Start by listening to God's Word again.

Out of this overall project comes the 9Marks series of books. These volumes intend to examine the nine marks more closely and from different angles. Some target pastors. Some target church members. Hopefully all will combine careful biblical examination, theological reflection, cultural consideration, corporate application, and even a bit of individual exhortation. The best Christian books are always both theological and practical.

It's our prayer that God will use this volume and the others to help prepare his bride, the church, with radiance and splendor for the day of his coming.

Introduction

What is *community* in your church? A monthly fellowship night? The conversation that follows a Sunday service? Good friends who know you? Many of us equate *community* with small groups. Over the last few months, I've told friends of mine from Shanghai to Seoul to San Francisco that I'm writing about church community. Their reply: "You mean a book about small groups?" I suppose your definition of *community* flows largely from the ambition you have for it. And in writing this book, I want to both raise and lower your ambition for church community.

Raising the Bar

On the one hand, I want to raise the bar of what you envision church community to be. I appreciate small groups. But they only scratch the surface of what God intends to create in your church through community. Why? Of all the ways that the gospel changes this world, the community of the local church is the most obviously supernatural. Its witness even goes beyond this world. "The rulers and authorities in the heavenly places" sit up and take notice, says Paul (Eph. 3:9–10). In this book, I'll define local church community as a togetherness and commitment we experience that transcends all natural bonds—because of our commonality in Jesus Christ. Far from being a "nice to have" element of your church, community is core to who you are. Is this really something you can leave to small groups or a mentoring program?

Humility and Honesty

On the other hand, I want to lower your ambition for church community. That is, I want to lower your ambition for what *you can do* to create community in your church. Scripture teaches that the community that matters is community built by God. We may cultivate it, feed it, protect it, and use it. But we dare not pretend to create it. When in our hubris we set out to "build community," we risk subverting God's plans for our churches—and I'm afraid this is something we do all the time.

So what is the book you hold in your hand? It is not a method for building community that you should implement with expectation of immediate change. Instead, it's a set of biblical principles that can guide gradual change in your congregation over several years.

It's not a book that's simply about relational closeness or fulfillment. Instead, it's a book that attempts to focus on God's purposes for church community instead of our own.

It's not a "new" book, but a modern-day retelling of truths that have been discussed throughout church history, and especially in the centuries following the Protestant Reformation.

It's not just theory; it's come out of my own church's real-life struggles to shape a more biblical community.

It's not a how-to book that tells you to copy what worked in one church, as if that example were applicable for everyone. It's an exploration of what God's Word says about community—paired with practical advice for how you might work out these principles in your own local church.

Who Wrote This?

You've probably noticed that two authors are on the cover, but I've been writing in the first-person singular. "I" being Jamie Dunlop. Mark Dever and I planned this book out together. I wrote it. Then we worked through the finished copy until we agreed on every word. We put both names on the cover because I couldn't claim this as "my book" with any form of integrity. Let me explain the story of how it came to be, and you'll see why.

For the greater part of two decades, I've been a member of Capitol Hill Baptist Church where Mark Dever pastors in Washington, DC. I moved to DC in the late 1990s shortly after he began serving as pastor, and I joined the church. In fact, it was the first church I'd ever joined. I watched the church transform slowly, sometimes imperceptibly, into the type of community you'll read about in these pages. After a few years, my wife and I moved to San Francisco. We joined a wonderful Presbyterian church near our home. But a few years later, we moved back to Capitol Hill. Not because we couldn't find a good church in San Francisco. Certainly not because we enjoyed DC more than San Francisco. But we missed Capitol Hill Baptist Church. More than Mark Dever, more than his preaching, we missed the community that had grown up around that preaching. A few years after arriving back in DC, I began serving as one of the church's elders. And a few years after that, I left my job in business and joined the church's staff as an associate pastor.

This book is about the type of community that I've seen form in the congregation I've come to love. In that sense, this is Mark's book. The underlying principles, experiences, and approaches you'll see described—sometimes even the way things are phrased—are all his. He's been conducting the orchestra, so to speak; I've been in the recording booth. Of course, that analogy falls flat since God is the author of all good that happens in any of our churches. But you get my point. Frankly, having sat under this man's teaching for so long, it's sometimes hard to know exactly where his words and ideas end and mine begin.

Compelling Community is a result of our partnership in the gospel over many years. As a result, this isn't a book full of good ideas that have never been tried. Nor is it a book about "the Capitol Hill Baptist way of doing church." On the one hand, we have put everything you read here into practice in our own church. Mark and I have taken our own medicine. On the other hand, I've taken pains in this book to avoid merely telling you to do things the way we have. I've used our church as an example—but rested my advice in the Scriptures and not in my church's experience. I'm confident that these principles will and should work out differently in your church.

As you can imagine, we have many to thank for bringing this project to fruition. My wife, Joan, and Jonathan Leeman at 9Marks Ministries patiently worked through the manuscript with me. Isaac Adams, Andy Johnson, Matt Merker, Erik Hom, and Michael Lawrence all provided important ideas and feedback. Hinson Baptist Church in Portland, Oregon, kindly hosted my family while I was writing. And Capitol Hill Baptist Church provided me with time, encouragement, and motivation to tell this story.

Who Should Read This?

Finally, I want to add something about you, the reader. I've written this book for church leaders. If you're a pastor or a pastor-in-training, you'll find the book aimed squarely at you. If you're in another position of church leadership, especially as an elder, then you're also my intended audience. If you're not a church leader, you don't have to put the book down—but know that you'll need to translate as you read. Use the book to help you support your church's leaders, and to shape whatever future leadership you may exercise in your congregation.

I want this book to encourage you. I hope it reminds you of how important community is in your own church. I hope it sends you deep into the Scriptures to see how God intends that community to function—even if you disagree with me at times. And I hope it leads you to praise God for his glory in the local church. More than your prowess as a church leader, more than any advice I can give you in a book, the gospel of Jesus Christ has power to create community in your church that is evidently supernatural. And that community in your church is part of what will propel both you and me into praise forever around his throne.

With that end in mind, please read, think, and worship.

Part 1

A Vision for Community

1

Two Visions of
Community

Two churches in my neighborhood offer a study in surprising similarity.

One church is a theologically liberal congregation; the other is the theologically conservative church where I pastor. Both started meeting in 1867. Both grew considerably with the city of Washington, DC, in the years surrounding the Second World War. Both struggled as the surrounding blocks were decimated by a wave of race-charged rioting. By the late twentieth century, both congregations had dwindled in number and consisted largely of older commuters from the suburbs. In response, both purged their roles to remove members who no longer attended. The future of both was in question.

But then starting in the late 1990s, both began to grow. Both attracted young people who were moving into the city, and both re-grew roots into the neighborhood. For many years, the growth of both churches was roughly the same: the membership of one never strayed more than a hundred or so people from the other. Both congregations care for the poor in the neighborhood. Both buzz with activity on Sunday mornings and throughout the week. Both receive attention in the secular press for their tight-knit community.

But despite a similar history, these two churches could not differ more at their core. When I first moved to Washington in the 1990s, the pastor of this other church didn't call himself a Christian. He didn't believe in the atonement, didn't believe in physical resurrection, and, as he explained to me one day, wasn't even sure he believed in God! Whereas our church logo cites Romans 10:17 ("Faith comes from hearing"), theirs describes them as "the church of the open communion." Ours is a congregation centered on the historic Christian gospel. Theirs is a congregation, I would maintain, focused on an entirely different gospel. And yet both appear to thrive.

My point? You don't need God to "build community" in a church.

How to Build Church Community without the Gospel

Now, if you're reading this book you probably *do* believe in the gospel of Jesus Christ. You probably *do* believe in a holy God, in the reality of sin, in the power of the atonement. And beyond that, you likely hold the Bible to be the perfect Word of God. So for you, community without the gospel isn't a danger. Right?

That's exactly where I intend to challenge you. I think we build community without the gospel all the time.

Leave aside the theologically liberal church I just described. My concern for the evangelical church isn't so much that we're out to deny the gospel in fostering community. Instead, my concern is that, despite good intentions, we're building communities that can thrive regardless of the gospel.

I'll give you an example. Let's say that a single mother joins my church. Who is she naturally going to build friendships with? Who is naturally going to understand her best? Other single moms, of course. So I encourage her to join a small group for single moms, and sure enough, she quickly integrates into that community and thrives. Mission accomplished, right? Not quite.

What occurred is a *demographic phenomenon* and not necessarily a *gospel phenomenon*. Single moms gravitate to each other regardless of whether or not the gospel is true. This community is wonderful and helpful—but its existence says nothing about the power of the gospel.

In fact, most of the "tools" we use to build community center on something other than the gospel:

- *Similar life experience:* Singles groups, newly married Bible studies, and young professionals networks build community based on demographic groupings.
- *Similar identity:* Cowboy churches, motorcycle churches, arts churches, and the like are all gospel-believing churches with something other than the gospel at the core of their identity.
- *Similar cause:* Ministry teams for feeding the hungry, helping an elementary school, and combating human trafficking build community based on shared passion for a God-honoring cause.
- *Similar needs:* Program-based churches build community by assembling people into programs based on the similarity of their felt needs.
- *Similar social position:* Sometimes a ministry—or an entire church—gathers the "movers and shakers" in society.

I recognize this probably sounds ridiculous. In the space of a hundred words I've critiqued Bible studies for single moms, singles groups, and hunger ministries. But stick with me for a moment. Underneath all these community-building strategies is something we need to expose and examine with fresh eyes.

Let's go back to the small group for single moms. There's nothing wrong with wanting to be with people of similar life experience. It's entirely natural and can be spiritually beneficial. But if this is the sum total of what we call "church community," I'm afraid we've built something that would exist even if God didn't.

My goal in writing this book is not for us to feel guilty whenever we enjoy a friendship that would probably exist even if the gospel wasn't true. My goal is not to encourage churches to aim at some entirely unrealistic model of relationship where we never share anything in common but Christ. Rather, my goal is twofold:

1. To recognize that building community purely through natural bonds has a cost as well as a benefit. Often, we look at tools like the single moms small group and see only positive. But there is a cost as well: if groups like this come to *characterize* community in our churches, then our community ceases to be remarkable to the world around us.

2. To adjust our aspiration. Many relationships that naturally form in our churches would exist even if the gospel weren't true. That's good, right, and helpful. But in addition, we should aspire for many relationships that exist only because of the gospel. So often, we aim at nothing more than community built on similarity; I want us to aim at community characterized by relationships that are obviously supernatural. And by *supernatural* I don't imply the mystical, vaguely spiritual sense in which pop culture uses the term. I mean the very biblical idea of a sovereign God working in space and time to do what confounds the natural laws of our world.

Two Types of Community

In this book, I'll contrast two types of community that exist in gospel-preaching, evangelical churches. Let's call one "gospel-plus" community. In gospel-plus community, nearly every relationship is founded on the gospel *plus* something else. Sam and Joe are both Christians, but the real reason they're friends is that they're both singles in their 40s, or share a passion to combat illiteracy, or work as doctors. In gospel-plus community, church leaders enthusiastically use similarity to build community. But as a whole, this community says little about the power of the gospel.

Contrast this with "gospel-revealing" community. In gospel-revealing community, many relationships would never exist but for the truth and power of the gospel—either because of the depth of care for each other or because two people in relationship have little in common but Christ. While affinity-based relationships also thrive in this church, they're not the focus. Instead, church leaders focus on helping people out of their comfort zones to cultivate relationships that would not be possible apart from the supernatural. And so this community *reveals* the power of the gospel.

You can't physically see the gospel; it's simply truth. But when we encourage community that is obviously supernatural, it makes the gospel visible. Think of a kid rubbing a balloon against his shirt to charge it with static electricity. When he holds it over someone's head with thin, wispy hair, what happens? The hair reaches for the balloon. You can't see the static electricity. But its effect—the unnatural reaction of the hair—is unmistakable. The same goes for gospel-revealing community.

Yet gospel-revealing community isn't our first inclination, is it? Our tendency is toward gospel-plus community because it "works." Niche marketing undergirds so many church growth plans because it "works." People gravitate to people just like themselves. If I told you to take a church of two hundred and grow it to four hundred in two years, you'd seem foolish *not* to build community based on some kind of similarity.

A friend of mine recently received such a growth directive. He pastors the English-language congregation of an ethnically Chinese church, and the advice he received consisted nearly entirely of which type of similarity he should focus on. "You should be the church for second generationals." "You should be the church for young professionals." "You should stick with English-speaking people of Chinese descent." And so forth. If you want to draw a crowd, build community through similarity. That's how people work.

So is there anything wrong with this? Isn't this just a basic law of organizational development? Does it matter how we draw the crowd so long as once they arrive we tell them the gospel?

Yes. It does matter. When Christians unite around something other than the gospel, they create community that would likely exist even if God didn't. As a modern-day tower of Babel, that community glorifies *their* strength instead of God's. And the very earnest things they do to create this type of community actually undermine God's purposes for it. Gospel-plus community may result in the inclusive relationships we're looking for. But it says little about the truth and power of the gospel. To understand why, let's examine God's purposes for the local church in the book of Ephesians.

Supernatural Community Is God's Plan for the Church

What is God's plan for the local church? The apostle Paul lays it out in Ephesians chapters 2 and 3. It begins with the gospel, in 2:1–10. We were "dead in the trespasses and sins" (v. 1). But God "made us alive together with Christ" (v. 5). "For by grace you have been saved through faith. And this is not your own doing; it is the gift of God, not a result of works, so that no one may boast" (vv. 8–9).

But that gospel doesn't end with our salvation; it leads to some very disruptive implications. Implication number one: unity. As Paul writes of Jews and Gentiles at the end of chapter 2, God abolished the dividing wall of hostility "that he might create in himself one new man in place of the two, so making peace, and might reconcile us both to God in one body through the cross, thereby killing the hostility. And he came and preached peace to you who were far off and peace to those who were near. For through him we both have access in one Spirit to the Father" (vv. 15–18). Note that the gospel alone creates this unity: the *cross* is how Christ put to death their hostility. After all, what else could ever bring together two peoples with such different history, ethnicity, religion, and culture?

Now, what is the purpose for this unity between Jews and Gentiles? Skip down to chapter 3, verse 10: God's intent was "that through the church the manifold wisdom of God might now be made known to the rulers and authorities in the heavenly places."

Consider a group of Jews and Gentiles who share nothing in common except for a centuries-old loathing for one another. For a less extreme, modern-day parallel, think of liberal Democrats and libertarian Republicans in my own neighborhood. Or the disdain the Prada-shod fashionista feels for the Schlitz-swilling NASCAR crowd (multiplied many times over, of course). Bring them together into the local church where they rub shoulders on a regular basis, and things explode, right? No! Because of the one thing they *do* have in common—the bond of Christ—they live together in astonishing love and unity. Unity that is so unexpected, so contrary to how our world operates, that even the "rulers and authorities in the heavenly realms" sit up and take notice. God's plans are amazing, aren't they![1]

Gospel-revealing community is notable along two dimensions (see figure on p. 26). First, it's notable for its *breadth*. That is, it stretches to include such peoples as divergent as Jew and Gentile. As Jesus taught in the Sermon on the Mount, "If you love those who love you, what reward do you have?" (Matt. 5:46). One way in which this community glorifies God is by reaching people who, apart from supernatural power, would never unite together. Remember Ephesians 2:18: "For through him we both have access in one Spirit to the Father." Second, this community is notable for its *depth*. That is, it doesn't merely bring people together to tolerate each other, but to be so tightly committed that Paul can call them a "new humanity" (2:15) and a new "household" (2:19, NIV). Paul reaches for the natural world's deepest bonds—the bonds of ethnicity and family—to describe this new community in the local church.

Supernatural depth and breadth of community make the glory of an invisible God to be visible. This is the ultimate purpose statement

---

[1] How do we know that Paul is referring to a local church here and not just the universal church? Three reasons: (1) What is true of the heavenly assembly should also be true of the local assembly. Peter O'Brien puts it well in his commentary: "Since it was appropriate that this new relationship with the ascended Lord should find concrete expression in believers' regular coming together, that is, 'in church' (cf. Heb. 10:25), then the term here in 3:10 should probably be taken as the heavenly gathering that is assembled around Christ *and* as a local congregation of Christians" (*The Letter to the Ephesians*, Pillar New Testament Commentary [Grand Rapids, MI: Eerdmans, 1999], 246). (2) Much of the rest of the epistle will discuss relationships between believers in a local church. (3) The focus of 3:10 is the present, not an assembly someday in heaven. The assembly of Jews and Gentiles *today* is the local church. And each congregation points to the larger, grander assembly of all peoples in Revelation 7.

for community in the Ephesian church. This is the ultimate purpose statement for community in churches today. Is it the ultimate purpose for community in your church?

Two Dimensions of Community in Ephesians 2

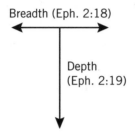

Breadth (Eph. 2:18)

Depth
(Eph. 2:19)

Let me summarize two foundational elements from Ephesians 2–3 before we move on:

1. *This community is characterized by commonality in Christ.* It's said that "blood is thicker than water." Our world's history is a long story of tribal conflict where no one is closer than those who are family. That is, with one critical exception of course: the local church. When two people share Christ—even if everything else is different—they are closer than even blood ties could ever bring them. Again, they are the family of God.

2. *If this community is not supernatural, it doesn't work.* By "work" I mean "fulfill God's plans for community." What if, instead of uniting around Christ, Jews and Gentiles figured out some nifty organizational trick for them to coexist? Would that make known "the manifold wisdom of God"? No. It would glorify *their* wisdom and *their* ability. And it could never approximate the breadth and depth of community described in Ephesians. What if Jewish Christians just loved Jewish Christians and Gentile Christians just loved Gentile Christians? Not a bad start . . . but compared to the community Paul describes in Ephesians, it says relatively little about the power of God in the gospel.

Does this mean that we should flee any relationships where we share Christ plus something else? No. God uses our sociological affinities. Every church has a certain culture, a certain feel, a certain majority. It would be dishonest to suggest otherwise, to say that a congregation shares *nothing* in common but Christ. Like is attracted to like, and that's a natural reality. There's nothing inherently wrong with people's comfort with the familiar. Nonetheless, an important question is, What are you going to build with? What tools are you going to use? Will you use the natural tools of "ministry by similarity"? Or, while recognizing our tendency toward similarity, will you set your aspiration on community where similarity isn't necessary—because of the supernatural bond of the gospel? As the apostle writes, "For the weapons of our warfare are not of the flesh but have divine power to destroy strongholds" (2 Cor. 10:4). The difference will show itself over time. When you build with natural tools, over time the natural divisions between people will become set in concrete. Use natural tools to reach middle-class whites, and over time your church will be middle-class white. But when you build with supernatural tools, over time those natural divisions begin to soften. An all-white church will, remarkably, slowly perhaps, become less all-white. This has been the story of my own congregation.

While recognizing our tendency toward similarity, we should aspire toward community where similarity isn't necessary—where no strand of similarity in the congregation explains the *whole* congregation. That kind of community defies naturalistic explanations.

God has great purposes for the community of your church: to safeguard the gospel, to transform lives and communities, to shine as a beacon of hope to the unconverted. Community that does this is demonstrably supernatural. It is not community designed around the gospel *plus* some other bond of similarity. It is community that *reveals* the gospel. Yet too often, community in our churches better testifies to our own prowess in niche marketing than to the supernatural at work. Why is this?

Pressure to Build Gospel-Plus Community

Quite simply, gospel-plus community seems more reliable than the supernatural community we see in Ephesians 2–3. We're sure we know how to make it happen. Compare community building to the breeding of some endangered species at the zoo. You could just let those black-footed ferrets have at it in nature's own special way and hope for progeny to blossom. But with so much at stake, you'd never leave it to chance, would you? So the zoo in my town is measuring timing, and temperature, and diet, and whatever else you can imagine to help black-footed ferrets breed as reliably as possible.

We have our own endangered species to protect: the community of the local church, and we know how important it is. Community makes people feel included. When people feel included, they stay and volunteer and give. When they don't feel included, they leave. So the growth of our churches and the apparent success of our ministries depend on effective community. With something that important at stake, it's understandable that we want it to be as reliable as possible. We want something we can control. Plus, we *do* want as many as possible coming to faith, and this is a good thing!

So what do we do? Like the ferret-breeding project, we seek community that is measurable and repeatable: community you can capture on a spreadsheet. We assign everyone to a life-stage small group. Or we slice and dice demographic segments to perfectly situate people in the resulting affinity groups. Or we narrow our "target market" until we reach precise homogeneity.

These pressures are nothing new. In his book *Revival and Revivalism*, Iain Murray traces the root of American Protestant liberalism to a tendency among Christians to seek seemingly supernatural results through entirely natural means.[2] The First Great Awakening of the 1730s and 1740s, Murray explains, was an example of genuine "revival." God chose to supernaturally bless the ordinary means of grace: the preaching of the Word of God and prayer. As time went

---

[2] Iain Murray, *Revival and Revivalism* (Edinburgh, UK: The Banner of Truth Trust, 1994).

on, however, God stopped blessing those means of grace to the same degree. And so the so-called Second Great Awakening of the early nineteenth century attempted to produce revival-like results through entirely mechanistic means—what Murray calls "revivalism." The book chronicles the destructive fruit of these tendencies in the American church; they are still alive and well today.

When we build gospel-plus community, we may get the inclusive relationships we're looking for. But aside from an unusual act of God, we will not achieve the supernatural breadth and depth of community that makes the world sit up and take notice. We build a demographic phenomenon, not a gospel phenomenon.

So how do we cultivate the type of community Paul describes in Ephesians?

A Book about the Shadow, Not the Substance

Oddly enough, we cultivate this kind of community by not paying it too much attention. And this is hard work. It is hard work to not worry and get impatient. It is hard work *not* to get in the way of the supernatural. But fostering church community is like learning to ride a bicycle. If you focus too much on the mechanics of what you're doing (left foot forward, right foot, quick! turn handles a little, lean to the right), you'll crash. But eventually we all realize that as we focus on the goal ahead, the riding happens.

In that sense, church community is the shadow, not the substance. It's not the thing we should focus on. To be sure, this *is* a book about cultivating community in a local church. We will explore how as a leader in your church you can help your congregation become fertile ground for the kind of organic, sharing-life relationships that we all hope to see in our churches. Yet as we do this, we must remember that community isn't the point. The point, the substance, is God. God is immortal. He "dwells in unapproachable light, whom no one has ever seen or can see" (1 Tim. 6:16). So how do we learn about him? Through his Word. And how do we perceive his glory? Primarily, through the church. The body of Christ is the fullness of God (Eph. 1:23) and the most visible manifestation of God's glory in this present age (Eph. 3:10). And so describing community in the local church is like describing the light radiating from the heavenly throne. The point is not the community; the point is God. Community is merely the effect.

Our new society of the church is not a *mutual* admiration society, but a *shared* admiration society. Our affection for each other is derivative. It derives from our worship of God—a God who saved us from a million different "communities" of this world to become his family. Our identify no longer stems from our families of origin, our professions, or our interests and ambitions, but the fact that we are in Christ. We are *Christians*. And so as an urban American of the professional class, I have more in common with my working class, rural, Sudanese brother in Christ than with my own non-Christian blood brother. Thus the song of heaven is praise for this culmination of Christ's exploits, that "by your blood you ransomed people for God from every tribe and language and people and nation" (Rev. 5:9). God and his glory in the church are the point, not the community we seek.

The Rest of This Book

In one sense then, nurturing Ephesians 3 community in a local church is simple. When the gospel is believed, the supernatural community described in the New Testament happens. Our problem is that our impatience for this all-important work of the Spirit leads us to construct it artificially. Consider how standard approaches affect depth and breadth of community:

- *Depth*: Instead of calling people to act out the supernatural depth of commitment to other Christians that is inherent to faith, we make our churches as low-commitment as possible for newcomers. "Slide on in," we say. "We've got no expectations." We hope that as they grow, these people will increase their commitment to one another. But, of course, what you win them with is how you'll keep them. Attract people as consumers, and you'll wind up with a church of demanding consumers. This may allow our people to feel some level of commitment quickly, but it compromises long-term depth of love for each other. And consumerism is the antithesis of the gospel of grace.

- *Breadth:* Since we attract people as consumers, there is no intrinsic commitment to others in our church. So we must manufacture that commitment. How? Through ministry by similarity. Instead of prophetically calling Christians to love those with whom they may have little in common but Jesus, we patch people into affinity groups where we know relationships will prosper. As a result, our church "community" is really pockets of independent, homogeneous communities that do not display the supernatural breadth God intends.

As you read through these chapters, you may hesitate at what I'm saying. "But wait," you might say. "If we don't have [insert name of ministry you use to attract people to your church], then how will people come? Don't you care about getting people into my church?" I do. Absolutely. But I'm concerned that the things we do to attract people can actually compromise our ability to nurture a supernatural community. And God intends that community to be profoundly more attractive than those things you're doing today. Yet to do this, you may need to rethink much of your ministry, such as your approach to small groups, your goals for Sunday services, or your membership policies. Then lay the groundwork for a community you're dependent on God to grow—a community whose attraction and beauty will reach to the heavens.

In all our efforts to build community, we so often destroy the very elements that should mark it out as a supernatural act of God. We're like King Saul, impatient with God's timing as he waited for an all-important sacrifice, deciding to do things our own way. The rest of this book shows how we as church leaders can foster biblical community *without* getting in the way.

Chapter 2 will examine what makes "supernatural community" *supernatural* in the first place. Then chapters 3 and 4 will assess how we can cultivate the two most distinctive marks of this supernatural community: its depth of commitment (chap. 3) and its breadth of diversity (chap. 4). With this foundation in place, the rest of the book will apply these principles to our preaching and prayer, how we encourage personal relationships, and how we address conflict and sin. Finally, the last two chapters will focus on stewarding the community God's given us—through evangelism and church planting.

Conclusion
Not All Community Is the Same

At the beginning of this chapter, I described the uncanny parallels of growth between the church where I pastor and another church that long ago rejected the Bible as its authority. Yet I don't believe for a moment that the community life of these two churches is in any way similar. One community can pretty much be understood by the world. Special, to be sure. But not unexpected. The other? The formerly non-Christian neighbors of mine, whom you'll meet in this book, would say it's something supernatural. It was community they could not explain as non-Christians, and yet found profoundly attractive despite the offense of the gospel at its core.

I'll close this chapter with some questions to help you assess your own attitudes toward church community.

1. How do you define "success" for the network of relationships in your church that we call community? How close is your definition to Ephesians 3:10 ("through the church the manifold wisdom of God might now be made known . . .")?
2. Are your goals and targets for nurturing community in the local church consistent with something that only God can create? Or do they push you to gospel-plus community that people can manufacture on their own?

3. Do you find yourself having to "sell" various programs and initiatives to your congregation? Or are you appealing to them in such a way as to move them away from a consumer mind-set?

4. What do you talk about with other church members outside of church? To what extent do casual conversations differ from what you'd expect to hear in a local bar/neighborhood picnic/Little League game?

5. How many of your friendships at church would likely exist even if you weren't a Christian?

This, then, is the thesis of this book: Authentic, gospel-revealing community with supernatural depth and breadth is a natural outgrowth of belief in God's Word. But we get impatient, building gospel-plus community that undermines God's purposes for the local church by compromising that same depth and breadth. So how do we work against our own worst tendencies and nurture biblical community in our churches? We start by examining exactly how God's community becomes "supernatural."

2

A Community Given by God

It's a chilling scene. Ezekiel is an exile in Babylon, but suddenly he sees the temple back in Jerusalem.[1] The glory of the Lord, which had filled the temple since the days of Solomon, is pictured as resting on a wheeled throne, and the throne is supported by flying cherubim. It begins to move. It departs from the Most Holy Place. It stops at the threshold of the temple. It advances again, rising upward from the temple and then moving over the east gate. Until it's gone. The glory of the Lord has left the temple. Unspeakable horror!

Yet nothing appears any different. The temple is still there. God's people are still there. Life continues unaltered. It's all the same.

At least for now.

Ezekiel's Vision in Your Own Church

What if the same thing happened to your church? Picture all the elements of community in your church: your main weekly gathering, the Lord's Supper, small groups, accountability relationships, conversations after church, and so forth. Now picture the Spirit of God and his supernatural power rising up and then departing from your congregation. What happens?

---

[1] Ezekiel 10

- Do some people immediately feel like they no longer belong? Or do they continue coming to church for mostly the same reasons they did before?
- Do some friendships instantly dissolve because no bond remains? Or do they survive because they were based on something other than the gospel in the first place?
- Do you notice a conspicuous change in the conversations people have in your small groups? Perhaps a new reluctance to engage in difficult talk about each other's lives? Or was the self-sacrifice in these relationships never dependent on God's Spirit to begin with?
- Do you begin to see a flood of requests for pastoral counseling because members are no longer bearing each other's burdens? Or have people always seen the pastoral staff as the "professionals" they call in a time of spiritual need?

I would hope that our churches would dissolve into chaos the moment God removed his supernatural power. But I fear that many of us have built church community in such a way that Ezekiel's vision could come true in our own day, and we would never notice the difference.

Consider the Boeing 747. Up until its introduction, all commercial airplanes could be flown on manual backup, just in case the hydraulic power failed. But with the advent of the superjumbo jet, technology was deemed sufficiently reliable, and this so-called "manual reversion" was no longer necessary. And so control of the 747—and most planes since—relies entirely on hydraulic power without any manual backup.

Is your church community flying on manual backup?

Have you built your community around the gospel *and* some other bonds? Or does it only hold together because of the supernatural power of Almighty God? Have you turned community-building into so much of a science that the supernatural has become optional?

Do these questions even matter?

They do. If community in your local church is not dependent on God's supernatural Spirit for its lifeblood, it is not *evidently* supernatural. If it is not evidently supernatural, it is counterfeit community. It's posing as biblical community but fails to accomplish its purpose. It fails to show off the wisdom of God to the world (Eph. 3:10).

To see this, I'll paint a picture from Scripture of what we lose when church community is *not* evidently supernatural. Then I'll finish the chapter by fleshing out exactly what makes a church community supernatural.

What We Lose When Community Isn't Evidently Supernatural

In the first chapter of this book, I argued that when we build church community primarily around something other than the gospel, we compromise God's purposes for the church. But what exactly are we giving up? Let's start with Jesus's command to his church at the end of the book of Matthew:

> All authority in heaven and on earth has been given to me. Go therefore and make disciples of all nations, baptizing them in the name of the Father and of the Son and of the Holy Spirit, teaching them to observe all that I have commanded you. And behold, I am with you always, to the end of the age. (28:18–20)

At the risk of oversimplification, there are two main thrusts of this Great Commission. We are to share the gospel with all nations— baptizing those who believe. In other words, we are to *evangelize*. And we are to teach each new generation of converts to observe all that Christ has commanded. In other words, we are to *disciple*.

When we cultivate local church community that is not evidently supernatural, we compromise both thrusts of our commission. We compromise our evangelism and we compromise our discipleship.

1. We Compromise Evangelism

Jesus's words in John 13 describe our power in evangelism: "By this all people will know that you are my disciples, if you have love for one another" (v. 35). And not just any love will do. The prior verse sets the standard for this love: "As I have loved you, you also are to love one another." The love that will mark believers as followers of Jesus is the same kind of costly, God-exalting, supernatural love that Jesus shows us. It's a love with the depth of the cross; it's a love with breadth to reach from heaven to earth. "We love because he first loved us" (1 John 4:19).

Now, does love exist in a community that's formed around something other than the gospel? Of course it does. Think of the kind of community you would find at Alcoholics Anonymous, the Rotary Club, or the Facebook page for your favorite band. There's friendship there—even affection—that's wonderful and real. But is this the inexplicable-without-God love that Jesus describes in John 13? No. It's natural love that the world recognizes. The love of John 13 and Ephesians 3 is *super*natural. When community in the local church defies natural explanation, it confirms the supernatural power of the gospel.

I wonder if this gospel-confirming ability of a local church community might explain an intriguing pattern in the book of Acts. As you read through Acts, you notice very quickly that nearly always, when the gospel first goes to a region, it's accompanied by what Luke calls miraculous signs (e.g., 2:43). These signs beg for explanation (e.g., Acts 2:12), and the explanation is the gospel. The book begins with the sign of tongues at Pentecost as the gospel is first preached in Jerusalem. Then the gospel goes to Samaria, and Luke tells us that "the crowds with one accord paid attention to what was being said by Philip when they heard him and saw the signs that he did" (8:6). Peter takes the gospel to Lydda and Joppa—where in both cities miracles confirm the words of the gospel (9:35, 42). And Paul's first missionary journey follows the same pattern, with supernatural signs in Cyprus (13:12), Iconium (14:3), Lystra (14:11), and so forth. The exception to the rule, incidentally, is in Pisidan Antioch where no signs are reported and he shakes the dust off his feet as he leaves (13:51).

But when the narrative revisits these cities—once local churches exist—the reports of miraculous signs stop. Instead, Luke limits his writing to two topics: the further preaching of the gospel and the strengthening of the church (e.g., Acts 8:25; 9:31; 14:22; 16:4; 18:23; 20:2). Is it possible that signs happen and we're just not told? Certainly. But if this pattern does exist, why does it exist? The Scriptures don't tell us. But here's my hypothesis: These miraculous signs were a temporary means of confirming the truth of the gospel. Temporary, that is, until the permanent miraculous means of confirmation was up and running: the local church. When the gospel first enters a region, the Spirit enables miraculous signs. Once the gospel takes root, the Spirit enables miraculous community.[2] This is John 13:35 in practice: evangelism that's empowered by gospel-confirming community. When we compromise the supernatural nature of that community, we compromise our evangelism.

2. We Compromise Discipleship

But evangelism isn't the only casualty. Community that is not evidently supernatural also compromises discipleship.

"Heresy is better than schism," said the Episcopal bishop of Virginia in 2004.[3] His comment targeted Bible-believing conservatives who were leaving the denomination after the consecration of a gay bishop. In many ways, that has been the rallying cry of the theological liberally, mainline church through much of the last century. In response, evangelicals sometimes view all calls for unity as the back door to liberalism. But according to the New Testament, both assumptions are misguided. Unity and truth are symbiotic. They cannot exist without each other.

In Matthew 28, Jesus commanded us that we should teach his

---

[2] First Corinthians 14 is the one New Testament example where miraculous signs occur within a church while confirming the truth of the gospel (v. 22). But even then, their *primary* purpose is to build up the miraculous community of the local church (v. 26).

[3] Julia Duin, "Heresy Better Idea Than Schism?" *The Washington Times*, January 31, 2004.

disciples "to observe all that I have commanded you." We are to stay faithful to Jesus's teaching ourselves, and then entrust it to those who come after us (cf. 2 Tim. 2:2). In Ephesians 4, we see this command in action:

> And he gave the apostles, the prophets, the evangelists, the shepherds and teachers, to equip the saints for the work of ministry, for building up the body of Christ, until we all attain to the unity of the faith and of the knowledge of the Son of God, to mature manhood, to the measure of the stature of the fullness of Christ, so that we may no longer be children, tossed to and fro by the waves and carried about by every wind of doctrine, by human cunning, by craftiness in deceitful schemes. Rather, speaking the truth in love, we are to grow up in every way into him who is the head, into Christ, from whom the whole body, joined and held together by every joint with which it is equipped, when each part is working properly, makes the body grow so that it builds itself up in love. (vv. 11–16)

Look at verse 14 again: "that we may no longer be children, tossed to and fro by the waves and carried about by every wind of doctrine, by human cunning, by craftiness in deceitful schemes." This is discipleship in action: stability in doctrine, resistance to false teaching, and a perseverance to observe all that Jesus commanded us, no matter what may come.

It's faithful teachers whom God uses to preserve our discipleship of Jesus, right? No! Not exactly. Look closely at the chain of cause and effect in the passage. It begins with Christ, who gives us ministers of the Word (v. 11). But these leaders don't guard us directly.[4] Instead, they are "to equip the saints for the work of ministry, for building up the body of Christ" (v. 12). The focus is on the congregation. Now, what does being "built up" look like? See verse 13: "until we all attain to the unity of the faith and of the knowledge of the Son of God,

---

[4] I don't intend by this to suggest that church leaders are not sometimes called to directly combat false teachers and false teaching (Acts 20:28–31; Titus 1:9). But while important, this is reactive in nature. The normal way that doctrine is positively protected is by equipping the congregation.

to mature manhood, to the measure of the stature of the fullness of Christ." That's what finally completes this golden chain that results in unshakable discipleship. Christ gives us leaders. They prepare the congregation for service. As a result, the congregation grows in unity and maturity. And it is through this congregational strength that we will resist being "carried about by every wind of doctrine" (v. 14).

Creeds, confessions, and statements of faith are useful. Denominational accountability is beneficial. Sound public teaching is invaluable. But nothing safeguards the gospel quite like the supernatural community of faith that gospel preaching produces. Lose what is supernatural about that community and, I fear in a generation or so, you lose the gospel.

In a sermon on a similar passage, Colossians 2:2–4, Pastor Michael Lawrence put it like this:

> To some extent, the postmodernists are right. There is a social character to knowledge, a community aspect to our perception of reality. That's why culture is so powerful. It shapes our perception of what is true, what is plausible. In a fallen world, culture becomes a plausibility structure for unbelief, for the denial of God and the exaltation of self. That is why the apostles are so concerned about the unity of the local church. The church is a counterculture, an alternative plausibility structure for faith.[5]

Christian community makes faith plausible. When I am tempted to believe this world's lies, community helps me remember that God's truth is perfect. Repeat that return to faith after a moment of doubt or temptation a dozen times over, and you have a typical week in my life. Repeat it hundreds of times, and you have a faithful week in the life of a church. Repeat it a million times over, and the gospel is preserved for the next generation. We are to "hold fast the confession of our hope without wavering" (Heb. 10:23) as we "stir up one another to love and good works" (v. 24), which is why we must never

---

[5] Michael Lawrence, *What Else Do You Need for Unity?*, May 1, 2011, http://hinsonchurch.org/gatherings/sermons/category/what-else-do-you-need.html.

neglect to meet together (v. 25). The local church is God's mechanism for protecting an unadulterated gospel. That's why Paul can call the church "a pillar and buttress of the truth" (1 Tim. 3:15).

OK, you might say, I understand that Christian community is part of preserving our discipleship of Christ. But won't any Christian community do? Can't my church running club do that? Or my Christian friends from my college days? What does this have to do with the "supernatural" community of the *local church*?

Think for a moment of those dimensions of breadth and depth in community that I mentioned in chapter 1. Let's evaluate them for an individual whose main Christian community is his friends from college. They've got lots in common, so they're pretty close. But commitment to each other isn't necessarily any deeper than the natural affinity that they share. Contrast that with a Jewish and Gentile believer in the Ephesian church. They've got little in common from a worldly standpoint. So, somewhat counterintuitively, the depth of their commitment to one another is much more profound. Rather than depending on natural affinity, it depends on the rock-solid love of Christ. You *may* have that depth of commitment with your friends from college, but not necessarily—since there are many more shallow reasons to be committed to one another. In a local church where believers commit to each other out of obedience to Christ, there is a depth of commitment that empowers courage to speak the truth in love (Eph. 4:15). In a group of friends from college where depth of relationship stems from natural affinity, there is no such guarantee.

The "college friends" type of community fails in its lack of breadth as well. In Ephesians 4:16, Paul explains how the golden chain I described functions: "when each part" of the body "is working properly." But when some parts are missing, how is this to happen? According to Paul, we need the *whole* body to preserve our doctrine, not just the parts we're most comfortable with. We need people who are different from us to keep us faithful to the gospel.

Why does your church exist in the first place? Certainly a key part of its purpose is to "go therefore and make disciples of all nations, baptizing them in the name of the Father and of the Son and of the Holy Spirit, teaching them to observe all that I have commanded you." Your church may accomplish many things without supernatural community. But it will be severely hindered in accomplishing the mission given by our Master and Maker.

What Makes Community Supernatural?

In case you've lost count, I've now used the word *supernatural* twenty-two times in this chapter. But I've not actually unpacked what it looks like, have I? This is often a problem in Christian circles. Phrases like "supernatural love," "doing things in God's strength," and "relying on Christ" get thrown around a lot—without much precision as to exactly what they mean. Tell a new Christian to "just lean on Jesus" and she nods her head vigorously, having absolutely no idea what she should do differently when she wakes up tomorrow.

The same applies to our discussion of "supernatural community." I've argued that the community of the local church should be supernatural in its depth and breadth. I defined *supernatural* in chapter 1 as the biblical idea of God working in space and time to do what confounds the natural laws of our world. But unless we understand exactly how community becomes supernatural, we have little hope of living out a biblical vision for the local church. Which leads to some remarkable words of Jesus.

In Luke 7, a sinful woman washes Jesus's feet with her tears and anoints them with perfume—to the horror of Simon, the watching Pharisee. Jesus responds by telling a parable about how a man who is forgiven a great debt loves his creditor more than a man forgiven a small one. Then he sums everything up in one statement: "Therefore I tell you, her sins, which are many, are forgiven—for she loved much. But he who is forgiven little, loves little" (v. 47).

Jesus's words capture the Pharisee's self-righteousness and turns it on its head. The Pharisee thought he was forgiven by God because of how well he loved God. And at first, that appears to be exactly what Jesus is saying: "her sins, which are many, are forgiven—for she loved much." We love people so that God will love us.

Yet as Jesus continues, we realize that's not his point at all. "But he who is forgiven little, loves little." Love doesn't cause forgiveness. It's the other way around, isn't it? Forgiveness is what causes love! That was the whole point of Jesus's parable. The late biblical scholar G. B. Caird summed this up well: "Her love was not the ground of a pardon she had come to seek, but the proof of a pardon she had come to acknowledge."[6] And so Jesus reassures her: "Your faith has saved you; go in peace" (v. 50).

Our love is proportional to our understanding of forgiveness. And because our forgiveness is supernatural, we have ability as Christians to love God supernaturally.

Further, to love God is to love other Christians. There is no exception to that rule. "If anyone says, 'I love God,' and hates his brother, he is a liar" (1 John 4:20). Thus John's earlier statement: "We love because he first loved us" (4:19). Having stripped everything else away, this is the iridescent, radioactive core of supernatural community in the local church. Supernatural *forgiveness* drives supernatural *love*. Let's take each of these in turn.

1. Supernatural Forgiveness

Christians are those whose sin is forgiven through the atoning death and resurrection of Jesus Christ. What makes our forgiveness supernatural? The fact that, apart from the miraculous, it is impossible. Enter the doctrine of sin. Our voluntary rebellion against a good and holy God has offended his perfect justice and provoked his just wrath against us. We are, as an old creed puts it, "by nature utterly void of that holiness required by the law of God, positively inclined to evil; and therefore under just condemnation to eternal ruin, without defense or excuse."[7]

---

[6] G. B. Caird, *Saint Luke* (1963; repr., Harmondsworth, Middlesex, England: Penguin, 1987), 115.
[7] The New Hampshire Confession, 1833. See Phillip Shaff, ed., *The Creeds of Christendom* (1931; repr., Grand Rapids: Baker, 1998), 3:743.

Our most fundamental problem is *not* that we lack meaning in life. It is *not* that we feel unfulfilled, unsatisfied, or unknown in community—or any of the other things we so often try to "sell" in our evangelism.

Our problem is sin. Our sin is heinous. And our salvation is not conceivable by any human imagination. If we have transgressed against the justice of an infinitely good and holy God—and what is more, if we have done so because we want to be god in his place—what are we to do? If God overlooks our sin, he ceases to be good. If he judges us, we are condemned to hell. And yet, as that marvelous verse in 2 Corinthians describes, "For our sake he made him to be sin who knew no sin, so that in him we might become the righteousness of God" (5:21). The miracle of the atonement is that there *is* a way for God to be both just and the one who justifies sinners (to paraphrase Rom. 3:26). Mercy and justice met when the sinless Son of God was, impossibly, sacrificed on our behalf. Our forgiveness as Christians is profoundly supernatural.

2. Supernatural Love

We love God to the extent that we understand his forgiveness. And, of course, to love God is to love those around us. What Jesus states in Luke 7 might be called an inviolable law of the spiritual universe. Those who have been forgiven much *will* love much. There are no exceptions. To quote 1 John again: "for he who does not love his brother whom he has seen cannot love God whom he has not seen" (4:20). Our love for each other is the visible sign that we grasp the love of an invisible God.

A cold heart that does not love suggests one of two things. Either it has never been forgiven, or it does not appreciate the depth of its forgiveness. In fact, much of our growth in Christ is simply growth in our understanding of what Christ has done for us.

We can never be forgiven more than we are at the moment of our salvation. Yet as we better understand our sin, and as we better understand the cross, we better understand our forgiveness—which flows out as more love. So what is supernatural about love within a local church community? This love is empowered not by the lovability of others or our own goodness, but by supernatural forgiveness in Christ at the cross.

Supernatural community in a local church is this principle being worked out hundreds of times each week. The people in our churches understand their sin. They understand the seeming absurdity—and yet reality—of forgiveness in Christ. That spark burns into love for God, which in turn creates love for others. So they love not in their own human strength, but in the supernatural strength of the one who loved them first.

Conclusion
Two Guiding Principles

A congregation doesn't love like this by themselves, however. They do this under the watchful care of church leaders. And so as church leaders, we face countless decisions that can either feed supernatural community in our churches or detract from it. Choose this ministry leader or that one? Should small groups be open to visitors or not? How can I help that brother who seems isolated? As you face real-life questions like these with an eye toward nurturing supernatural community, here are two guiding principles to keep in mind.

1. Regeneration Precedes Community

Many pastors realize several months into ministry that a good portion of their new church is probably composed of non-Christians. These people may have been at the church their whole lives, but they give little evidence of being born again. In this case, community is premature. Nothing I've described in this chapter is possible for someone who is not in Christ. In fact, one sign that many in your congregation are not regenerate is how hard you have to work to motivate them. If an attractional ministry has gathered a congregation of Christians in name only, you will have to manipulate or coerce them into acting like followers of Jesus.

My advice? Preach the gospel—from the pulpit and in private conversation. Meet up with the members of your church to understand where they're at spiritually. Ask church members to understand and agree to your church's statement of faith. Encourage those who do seem to be Christians to study Scripture with those who are not. Eventually, as their lives' fruit reveals the true state of their hearts, you will likely remove some of them from membership. That will be to their lasting benefit if God shows them mercy (1 Tim. 5:24; 1 Cor. 5:5). But hold off any ambition to see real biblical community built across the entire church membership.

You will feel pressure to resort to the gospel-plus community-building tools I described in the first chapter. But if you give in, all you will do is to make your church more comfortable for those who are Christians in name only. You want a church community that is engaging for earnest Christians—and for earnest unbelievers investigating the faith. But avoid any kind of community that will encourage nominal Christians to maintain their blithe disinterest in life's ultimate questions. You must believe that because supernatural community is God's plan as instructed in Scripture, it is the best means to reach the unbelievers in your church. Be patient for now, even at the cost of letting community languish, and focus on preaching the gospel. At times, this will take years to come to fruition—but it is well worth it.

Rather than trying to win your princess by dressing up the ugly toad you've been given, let supernatural forgiveness turn that toad into prince charming. And then the princess will come running. The rest of this book assumes largely regenerate membership in the local church.[8]

2. Theology Precedes Practice

Many Christians believe that rich community is allergic to a deep interest in theology. After all, theology divides; community unites,

---

[8] I say "largely regenerate" because in no church can we ever be fully confident that every member is a Christian. This book doesn't assume some perfected state where every member is a Christian. Rather, it assumes a church where we take care to restrict membership to those who give evidence of regeneration—even if in some cases we find out later we were wrong. For more wisdom on this issue, see *Church Membership* by Jonathan Leeman (Wheaton, IL: Crossway, 2011).

right? If you've been following what I've written so far in this chapter, you will recognize the absurdity of this assertion. Remember, our love isn't proportional to our forgiveness; it's proportional to our *understanding* of forgiveness. If someone has been forgiven by Christ's supernatural sacrifice at the cross—and yet that person never explores the depths of his sin and the miracle of the atonement—his love will remain tepid. It is impossible to know too much about God and his love for us in Christ. If someone is into theology and not into loving others, the problem isn't that he's spent too much time learning about God; it's that he never took to heart what he learned. In fact, 1 John warns he may not even be a believer at all.

Supernatural community begins with sound theology. It is unapologetic about the sinfulness of sin. It is honest about God's personal wrath in a personal hell—rather than making hell seem like a logical consequence of his justice that even he's embarrassed by. It glories in the miracle of the atonement—how at the cross something so horrific could achieve something so beautiful. And in keeping with Christ's resurrection from the dead, it expects transformed lives as a result. The rest of this book assumes a church that proclaims these truths with love, with clarity, and without apology.

So what *can* we do to help this supernatural love take root in our churches? For one, we can create an expectation of deep commitment among church members.

3

Community Runs Deep

Ours is the age of the consumer. If one thing unites church leaders everywhere, it is frustration over a consumerist mentality. A recent feature in *Leadership Journal* asked pastors of churches from all corners of evangelicalism—seeker-sensitive to modern liturgical, megachurch to house church—how they combat consumerism in worship.[1] The answers? "Encourage small groups." "Have great music." "Use humor." "Try hard to be un-hip." "Rely on the Word to change people." These are exceedingly divergent answers, as you would expect from exceedingly divergent perspectives. But despite disagreement over the solution, none of these leaders questioned the problem. Consumerism is dangerous. Healthy churches need providers, not consumers. After all, if consumers fill our pews, who's going to turn on the lights? Who's going to staff children's ministry? Who's going to welcome people at the door? Advocating for commitment in a local church would seem as controversial as advocating for Jesus.

---

[1] Eric Reed, "Human Hands, God's Fingertips," *Leadership Journal* (Spring 2011), http://www.christianity today.com/le/2011/spring/humanhands.html.

Comfort-Based Commitment

Yet the very strategies we use to battle consumerism often feed into it. Let me explain.

Every church seeks commitment from its members. Churches want people who say, "You can count on me," instead of sitting back and asking, "What have you done for me lately?"

How do people commit to a local church? Generally, in the same way they decide to commit to anything else in this world. Consider how you might commit to buying Apple products. At first, a Mac is just another computer and an iPad is just another screen. But maybe you end up borrowing your friend's Mac to check an e-mail and you realize that the screen doesn't freeze as much as it does on your PC. You'd hardly call yourself a committed Mac user yet, but you're intrigued. So when your PC finally dies, you decide to give Apple a try—even if their machines cost a bit more. Then your friends notice you're using a Mac, and it's your trendiest friends who seem most excited. After you get used to the Mac, you fall in love with how intuitive everything is. And how much better you fit in when you're working in a coffee shop. Suddenly, you realize you've been talking a lot about your Mac because your great-aunt gives you an iPad for Christmas, which becomes an inseparable part of your brain. Before long, you're going to Mac conventions, dressing your kids in Apple gear, and wearing blue jeans and black turtlenecks everywhere you go. You've committed (probably a little too much) to Apple.

And how did it happen? Well, it didn't happen all at once, and you certainly didn't intend on becoming an Apple fanatic. But the further you got in, the more attractive it looked, until you were in pretty deep.

That's similar to how commitment works in the church. We begin by emphasizing that we have no expectations for newcomers, and we advertise church as a great place to learn the Bible, educate your kids, find community, and feel close to God. Then, as people take a step closer into the church and feel more comfortable, we encourage them to make a slightly deeper commitment.

Think for a moment of the different ways this plays out:

- Commitment through ministry experience: Service in the local church is a tool to get people interested so that they'll commit further. Join the praise team, and hopefully as you get a taste for ministry, you'll sign up for more.
- Commitment through small groups: We encourage small groups as a gateway to the church. Join a small group, and if you like it, consider moving on to make deeper commitments elsewhere in the church.
- Commitment through counseling: If we can address people's problems through pastoral counseling, they'll become interested in making a larger commitment to the church. And so counseling also serves as a gateway to deeper commitment.

The model in view is commitment as a process. I'm going to call it "Comfort-Based Commitment." Over time, as people see the church community meeting their needs, they become more comfortable. As they become more comfortable, they commit more deeply. As a result, our instinct is to smooth the path into our churches and to highlight the benefits of getting further involved. Hopefully as people settle in, they'll act less like consumers and more like providers.

That's how we think about commitment in our churches. You can see how common this is by how church software works. Across vendors, church database programs share one goal: to track the "assimilation process" (as it's known)—where people move from casual attender to committed member—by way of service opportunities, small groups, leadership roles, etc. Why is software designed this way? Because that's what we want! That's what we'll pay for.

Trouble in Paradise

And yet . . . as common as the comfort-based mentality is, it doesn't foster the church community we desire. Specifically, it has three problems:

1. It tells at best a half-truth about what it means to be a Christian. And as theologian J. I. Packer once remarked, "A half-truth masquerading as the whole truth becomes a complete untruth."[2] The New Testament doesn't treat Christians as consumers who need to become providers as they mature. Instead, it assumes that all Christians act as providers—that all Christians commit deeply to a local church in ways that are meaningful, sometimes painful, and quite deliberate. Take the passage of 1 John I cited in the previous chapter as an example. In quite black-and-white terms, John insists that to follow Christ is to love other Christians.

> We love because he first loved us. If anyone says, "I love God," and hates his brother, he is a liar; for he who does not love his brother whom he has seen cannot love God whom he has not seen. And this commandment we have from him: whoever loves God must also love his brother. (1 John 4:19–21)

For John, love between believers isn't a sign of maturity; it's a sign of saving faith. If people's church involvement is motivated entirely out of what's in it for them, where do they fit in 1 John's portrait of a Christian? Even though churches built around Comfort-Based Commitment seek to battle consumerism, they still attract people as consumers. And when we attract people as consumers, we fail to tell them the whole truth about what it means to follow Christ.

"But be realistic!" you might say. "People *are* consumers. How else are you going to attract them if you don't attract them as consumers? Isn't it natural that we'd attract them as consumers, and then move them on from there?" That brings us to problem number two.

2. Comfort-Based Commitment doesn't necessarily demonstrate the gospel's power. Remember: biblical church community should reveal something supernatural about our motives and love. Yet simply easing people down the path of Comfort-Based Commitment produces a commitment no different from commitment to any other

---

[2] J. I. Packer, *A Quest for Godliness* (Wheaton, IL: Crossway, 1990), 126.

civic-minded organization. I remember my non-Christian realtor's reaction when he began attending my church. As he got to know us, one particular characteristic grabbed his attention: this was community built around something other than mutual self-interest. "I've always thought that evangelical Christians just didn't get it," he remarked. "Mormons and Jewish synagogues have these tight-knit communities—and they're an amazing business resource for them. Evangelicals have all the same community and I've always wondered why they don't put it to work. But now I'm realizing there's something here that's so much more than that." As he began to investigate that "something" beyond quid pro quo relationships, he began studying the Gospel of Mark with a member of my church. I wish I could say he was saved and baptized into our church; unfortunately, his interest in religion eventually dried up. But his observation was astute. When commitment in a local church transcends the benefits we receive from it, it points to something deeper.

3. Relationships thrive on commitment. A few years ago, a college freshman named Kaitlin visited my church. She liked our teaching but was put off by our focus on membership—because it felt wrongly exclusive and demanding. "Why do I need to sign a piece of paper to love people in my church?" What she wanted were authentic relationships, not a bunch of formalities. A few years passed while she visited various churches, until she finally settled back at my church—and joined! Why the change of heart? It turned out that the thing she found offensive—membership—was essential to the thing she craved: authentic relationships. As she visited church after church that downplayed the commitment they required, she found church after church where relationships proved shallow. But as she interacted with her college friends who had committed to churches that made a big deal of membership, she heard about the community she so wanted.

Kaitlin discovered that commitment is foundational to community. Initially, she wanted a church where she could slip in gradually to see if the community felt right for her. But churches that appealed to her as a consumer were (not surprisingly) full of consumers. After all, if you attract people by appealing to them as consumers, you'll most likely retain them as consumers. And consumerism stifles authentic relationships.

Calling-Based Commitment

That's what Comfort-Based Commitment looks like. But a church built on the commitment of church membership is different. It requires commitment *up front*: you bind yourself to a group of Christians that, frankly, you don't actually know that well. When a person is baptized, he or she is making an *up-front* commitment to follow Christ—and much of that is a commitment to love other believers. Church membership attaches that general commitment to a specific group of people. Your commitment to them doesn't stem from feelings of attachment or comfort or belonging (though I hope those feelings follow). Instead, it's a commitment you make because doing so is part of following Jesus. As Kaitlin found out, something everyone is talking about—authentic community—is bound up in something people rarely ever talk about: church membership.

Instead of Comfort-Based Commitment, I want us to aspire to something I'll refer to as Calling-Based Commitment. We commit to other believers in the local church simply because it's part of God's *calling* us into his family. It's what it means to be a Christian. Take the passage I cited earlier from 1 John. It starts with our salvation: "He first loved us." Then it continues into our love for other Christians. "Whoever loves God must also love his brother." *Every* person loved by God in this salvific sense loves other Christians. There are no exceptions. And that means we should stop viewing commitment to a local church as a *process* and start viewing it as an *event*. The event is our salvation, and commitment is something that inevitably follows—not something that merely happens as we mature.

But isn't it good and right for us to increase in our love for other believers? Of course. All over the New Testament you'll find prayers for exactly that. Take 1 Thessalonians 3:12 as one example: "May the Lord make you increase and abound in love for one another and for all, as we do for you." Growth in commitment is good. But growth *into* commitment is unbiblical. As I'll detail in a few paragraphs, the foundational level of commitment that every believer should make to a local church is quite profound. I'm not arguing that we make *all* of our commitment to a local church up front—but that we should make a *significant* commitment up front.

There's nothing wrong with Comfort-Based Commitment in and of itself. The problem is when it becomes our main tool for building community in the local church. If we lower our initial expectations for newcomers[3] to near zero and rely on Comfort-Based Commitment to kick in over time, we will have community that is consumerist, relationship-light, and not-that-different-from-the-world. Instead, we should *call* true believers to commit in deep and meaningful ways to the local church community and then increase their love from there. This is what God calls them to do—even before they've developed any particular affection for our community. Then we will find a community that's honest about what it means to follow Christ and that serves as a rich catalyst for Christian relationships.

The Bible Assumes Commitment That Is Significant

But what exactly does this commitment look like? What should we expect to see in all sinners saved by grace? The answer is found across the pages of Scripture—and part of that answer is a commitment of surprising significance. Let's walk through the ways that the Bible calls *all* Christians to commit to one another in a local church.

---

[3] I have in mind *Christians* who are newcomers.

Love One Another Deeply and Sacrificially

Romans 12:13–16 tells us to "contribute to the needs of the saints and seek to show hospitality. . . . Rejoice with those who rejoice, weep with those who weep. Live in harmony with one another." If my wife and I are unable to get pregnant, we should rejoice when our fellow church member gets pregnant. If I just got a new job, I should weep with my fellow church member who lost his. I should give of my money, my time, and my home to care for others in my church—simply because they are *God's people*. A small way I've seen that in my own church is when members show up for the wedding of another member they don't actually know that well. You can imagine the conversation with other guests at the reception: "So how do you know Maurice and Tonya?" "We're members at the same church." "OK, but how do you know them?" "I guess I don't that much—but since we go to church together, I wanted to support them by attending their wedding." "Really? Even though you don't know them? Why?" Enter the gospel.

Assemble Regularly with One Another

Hebrews 10:25 tells us that ours is a life of "not neglecting to meet together, as is the habit of some, but encouraging one another, and all the more as you see the Day drawing near." To be a Christian is to join with other Christians on a regular basis as the local church, becoming those in Matthew 18:20 who "are gathered in my name."

Encourage One Another

Look again at Hebrews 10. Verse 24 tells us to "consider how to stir up one another to love and good works"—something that must take place primarily through the gatherings of verse 25. As much as Christians are to meet together, they are to commit to encouraging one another.

Guard One Another

As it turns out, encouragement in the book of Hebrews is much more than brief compliments as we dash for the exits after a Sunday service.[4] In Hebrews 3:12–13 we see what encouraging one another really involves.

> See to it, brothers and sisters, that none of you has a sinful, unbelieving heart that turns away from the living God. But encourage one another daily, as long as it is called "Today," so that none of you may be hardened by sin's deceitfulness. (NIV)

Encouragement is an antidote to unbelief. To encourage means to strengthen each other's faith. It means being merciful to those who doubt (Jude 22). It means helping each other hold the shield of faith (Eph. 6:16). A commitment to encourage is a commitment to fight for faith together.

This responsibility to guard each other is given not only to church leaders, but to church members. Hebrews 3 was written for *all* Christians, not just their pastors. Similarly in 1 Corinthians 5, Paul rebukes the *entire* church for not acting when one of their own was immersed in unrepentant sin. And when false teachers began teaching a false gospel to the Galatian churches, Paul writes to the *entire* body of Christians, imploring them to act. To be sure, guarding each other against the self-deception of immorality and unbelief is something we do under wise and loving leadership (Titus 1:9). But ultimately, the New Testament gives responsibility for guarding one another to the entire church.

I could go on, but these four categories offer a useful starting point. The Bible assumes that all Christians love one another deeply and sacrificially. It assumes that all Christians assemble regularly with one another. It assumes that all Christians encourage one another to fight for faith. It assumes that all Christians guard one another—through difficult conversations and sometimes

---

[4] Throughout this book, I'm going to write as if your church meets on Sunday morning. I do that because this habit is normal for Christians around the world, following the example of the early church (1 Cor. 16:1–2; Acts 20:7) who gathered to celebrate Christ's resurrection on the first morning of the week. But please don't take this as an implied critique of your decision to meet at a different time than Sunday morning. The circumstances behind that decision will certainly vary among congregations.

through church discipline. In each case, the most basic level of commitment by a Christian to his church is surprisingly substantial.

But if we stop here, we still fall short of the New Testament's full vision of Christian love. Not only does the Bible envision commitment that is significant, it envisions commitment that is formalized.

The Bible Assumes Formalized Commitment

Recall Kaitlin's objection to church membership from earlier in this chapter: "Why do I need to sign a piece of paper to love people in my church?" Is the formal commitment of church membership an *essential* part of Christian love? And if the New Testament envisions some degree of formality, what difference does it make? To get to this question, let's go to 1 Corinthians 5. Paul writes:

> I wrote to you in my letter not to associate with sexually immoral people—not at all meaning the sexually immoral of this world, or the greedy and swindlers, or idolaters, since then you would need to go out of the world. But now I am writing to you not to associate with anyone who bears the name of brother if he is guilty of sexual immorality or greed, or is an idolater, reviler, drunkard, or swindler—not even to eat with such a one. For what have I to do with judging outsiders? Is it not those inside the church whom you are to judge? God judges those outside. "Purge the evil person from among you." (vv. 9–13)

The detail I want you to notice is the line separating the "inside" and the "outside" of the church (v. 12). Is this demarcation merely between those who physically assemble with the believers and those who don't? No, Paul assumes a few chapters later that non-Christians gather together with the church (1 Cor. 14:23–25). Instead, the line defines the church. On one side are those who call themselves believers and submit that profession to the judgment of the church. On the other side are those who may attend but who have made no such commitment. In fact, when Paul describes a church discipline case in 2 Corinthians 2:6 he writes, "For such a one, this punishment by the majority is enough." It seems this congregation made affiliation sufficiently formal that Paul could determine when "the majority" had acted.

Along similar lines, consider Jesus's injunction to "tell it to the church" in Matthew 18:17. In doing this, Jesus assumes that each of his followers would be part of a church. And he assumes a degree of authority that the congregation bears over the individual. All this points to a self-conscious relationship between believer and church. The believer understands who he is accountable to, and the church understands who it is accountable for. It understands who is "inside" and "outside," to use Paul's language.

Both of these passages are about church discipline; that's where Scripture speaks most clearly on the formality of commitment to a local church. After all, formality is generally invisible when things go well. When an auto manufacturer and its supplier get along and sales are flowing in, the contract gathers dust in a filing cabinet. But the moment a disagreement occurs, the formal contract takes center stage. We learn most about formality of commitment by observing in Scripture what happens when things go wrong.

But we also see the formalized nature of church commitment in the New Testament's teaching on church leadership. Take Hebrews 13:17 as an example: "Obey your leaders and submit to them, for they are keeping watch over your souls, as those who will have to give an account. Let them do this with joy and not with groaning, for that would be of no advantage to you." Which church leaders does Hebrews say that Christians should obey? Any that come along? No, they should obey the leaders of the church to which they belong. And for which Christians will these leaders someday give account to Christ? Any who come through the church door? No, they're responsible for the specific members of their church.

Pity the poor church leaders—in churches both large and small—

who will someday give account for flocks that are so amorphous that no one really knows who's inside the church. Pity the poor church attenders who never commit to obey a particular set of church leaders and instead attempt responsibility as their own shepherds— a responsibility they were never intended to fulfill.

Whether examining the Bible's teaching on church discipline or church leadership, it's clear that church commitment is a self-conscious decision. Believers know whom they're committing to; the congregation and its leaders know whom they're assuming responsibility for.

So what do you call this base level of Christian commitment? For the purposes of this book, I'll continue using Paul's imagery in 1 Corinthians, Ephesians, and Colossians of the local church as a body and us as its members. I'm going to call it membership. All Christians are to be meaningfully and self-consciously committed to a particular body of believers, acting as providers rather than as consumers. And this behavior doesn't exist to indicate that they are *mature* Christians, but that they *are* Christians.

Does this mean that every church must have a printed member-ship roll, membership classes, membership covenant, and so forth? Of course not. Membership will look different in different contexts. But however you do membership, you need to make it self-conscious. That is, when people join they understand the commitments they're making—and the rest of the church should understand their respon-sibility as well. In my own context, here's what has proved useful in accomplishing this:

Actions that clarify the responsibility new members take on when they join

- Before a person joins, we ask him or her to take six classes that explain what membership involves. We consider this a "truth in advertising" campaign—so new members will understand what this commitment involves and to whom they're committing.

- Before a person joins, he or she sits down with an elder for an hour to share his or her testimony, explain the gospel, and discuss what it looks like to be a member.
- We ask each new member to understand and sign our church covenant, a document that summarizes the biblical "one another" commands that I reviewed earlier in this chapter.

Actions that clarify the congregation's responsibility for its members

- We continually update a paper copy of a membership photo directory and encourage our members to pray through the entire membership over the course of each month.
- Before we share the Lord's Supper, we ask the members of the church to stand and read through the church covenant together—reminding us of what we've committed to do.
- When a new member joins, the elder who interviewed her gives a brief synopsis of her testimony to the whole congregation. Then we ask the congregation to vote on accepting that person into our church. One reason for the vote is to fulfill what we understand is the congregation's responsibility for determining who is part of the church (Matt. 18:17–19; 1 Cor. 5:12). But another reason for the vote is that it is a formal acceptance by the congregation to take responsibility to fold this person into our church family—and to make our lives open to her as relationships permit.

However you do this in your context, you must continually clarify that church membership means committing before we're comfortable—because of our calling by God.

Some churches fall short of this biblical vision because they are allergic to any kind of formality—and don't have membership at all. Other churches have membership, but don't manage it carefully. Theirs is not *meaningful* membership, and thus they do not call Christians to commitment that is in any way significant. And still other churches attempt the coexistence of meaningful membership with a consumer-focused "selling" of the benefits of church commitment.

In contrast to these shortcomings, we must call Christians to real discipleship of Christ: discipleship that involves significant, self-conscious commitment to the local church. Scripture has no other concept of Christian.

Formal Commitment Catalyzes Informal Commitment

But what difference does this formality really make? Clearly, the Bible sees informal commitment as of primary importance. So how does the formality of membership contribute to a culture of informal commitment between church members? To put it back in Kaitlin's words, how does a piece of paper help me love my church? Let me lay out three different ways.

1. *Formal commitment serves as affirmation of informal commitment.* The analogy of marriage is helpful. Here's how Tim Keller describes the marital application of this truth:

> When the Bible speaks of love, it measures it primarily not by how much you want to receive but by how much you are willing to give of yourself to someone. How much are you willing to lose for the sake of this person? How much of your freedom are you willing to forsake? How much of your precious time, emotion, and resources are you willing to invest for this person? And for that, the marriage vow is not just helpful but is even a test. In so many cases, when one person says to another, "I love you, but let's not ruin it by getting married," that person really means, "I don't love you *enough* to close off all my options. I don't love you enough to give myself to you that thoroughly." To say, "I don't need a piece of paper to love you" is basically to say, "My love for you has not reached the marriage level."[5]

While many discontinuities exist between marriage and church membership (e.g., joining one church doesn't "close off all my

---

options" to join another one in the future), the two are similar in how formal and informal commitment support each other. If someone says that they intend to fulfill all the "one another" commands in the context of your church but refuses to formally commit to doing so through membership, what kind of commitment do they actually intend to make? To extrapolate from Keller's language, their love for your church has not reached the membership level. Formal commitment clarifies who is making the decision to love your church as Scripture describes—and who is still weighing whether or not they really intend to follow Jesus.[6]

2. *Formal commitment makes informal commitment visible.* When I'm deciding whether to purchase a product from an unfamiliar online merchant, I pay a lot of attention to their certification. Are they part of the Amazon.com network? Approved by VeriSign? "Verified by Visa"? The formal commitments merchants have made to these online patrol officers assure me that they'll handle my personal information carefully. In the same way, formal commitment in a local church advertises the informal commitments someone's made. Let's say you walk up to someone you barely know in your church and say, "Hey, I noticed that we work a block from each other. How about we have lunch every other Thursday to study the Psalms?" In the "real" world, he'd look at you suspiciously and wonder if you're a sociopath. But since this person is a member of your church, the request isn't abnormal at all because when you became church members, you committed to care for each other. You can take a relational leap like this knowing that your church's culture of commitment will likely catch you. The formal commitment you make to each other is what makes visible the presence of informal commitment—so relationships can grow at a more rapid pace.

3. *Formal commitment makes informal commitment accountable.*

---

[6] Note that "formal" need not imply "written." Consider a small church in an environment of persecution. For security reasons, there may be no written membership list. Yet members still know quite clearly who has made the commitment and who has not. The words "church membership" are not in the Bible—but the principles clearly are. How we apply them will no doubt vary by situation.

Sometimes informal commitment proves powerless to counteract unrepentant sin; in these times we move from Matthew 18:16 ("take one or two others along") to 18:17 ("tell it to the church"). In these cases, formal commitment serves as God's final earthly barrier to self-deception. The church tells a professing Christian, "Based on the unrepentant sin in your life, we no longer have confidence that you really are a Christian." Could a congregation practice church discipline without the formal commitment of membership? I suppose so. But a lack of formal commitment to live under the discipline and authority of the church exacerbates an already difficult situation. Similarly, formal commitment protects a church culture from abuse. In some churches, issues of legitimate Christian freedom are trampled in the name of "wisdom" and discipleship veers toward a personality cult. It is more difficult to abuse authority in a local church when our responsibilities to each other are written out and discussed through the formality of church membership.

Those are three ways that formal membership supports informal commitment between believers. But for a moment, take a break from this line of argument and consider your own church. I think it's safe to say that you would like to see a culture of commitment grow up in your church. The question you need to answer is this: To what extent does your church's concept of formal commitment help or hinder a culture of informal commitment? Consider these questions:

- Does your church's practice of membership (or its equivalent) make clear the type of commitment someone is making when they join? Or is it unclear what being a member actually involves?
- Do your people know who has and has not made this formal commitment? Or is it invisible to all but church leaders?
- Does becoming a member change the practical reality of how a person relates to the rest of the congregation? Or for all practical purposes, can someone fully participate in your church community without ever making the commitments to other believers that the Bible calls them to make?

- Does your church's practice of membership create a safe place for relationships to blossom? Or does being a member say little about a person's commitment to the congregation?
- Does your church's practice of membership make clear that joining the church involves submission to the accountability and discipline of the church? Or is accountability to individuals and the full body never discussed in your church?

Near my house is the United States Botanic Garden—a glass-covered sanctuary built in 1933 for warm-weather plants. One of my favorite winter activities is to take the short walk with my family to the garden and feel the damp city chill give way to the warm rain-forest air of the main atrium. Think of church membership as that glass covering, standing against the cold world outside to establish the boundary conditions for a lush ecosystem of relationships in your church. Ultimately, if you want to create a culture of deep relationships in your church, you need a culture of commitment. And if you want a culture of commitment, you must consider carefully what biblical commitments people must make in order to fully participate in your church community.

Conclusion
Why Calling-Based Commitment Is So Countercultural

Does your pastor ever feel like the "chief sales officer" of your church? He spends his time drumming up support for the children's ministry, recruiting people for small groups, getting folks to sign up for the canned food drive, fund-raising, and generally trying to convince people to give more of themselves to the church. How exhausting! But this is where Comfort–Based Commitment inevitably leads. So why do we do things this way?

Because it's how people operate. Comfort-Based Commitment offers a familiar and appealing "try before you buy" mentality. Calling-Based Commitment, on the other hand, with meaningful and formal commitment that precedes deep relationships, offends. People want to form relationships on their own terms—not those handed down from above. After all, in its essence, "formal commitment to a local church" is just another way of saying "submission to authority." When we commit to a local church, we hand to other believers the authority to instruct us on how we should live our lives. And therein lies the problem. Our culture is deeply skeptical of authority. "Power corrupts, and absolute power corrupts absolutely," we quote.[7]

But the Bible tells us that a universal skepticism of authority isn't wise; it's satanic. The idea of distrusting authority didn't originate in our own generation but with the Serpent in the garden. The lie he planted in Eve's mind was that God cannot love us and say "no" to us simultaneously. That affection necessarily implies approval.

We must recognize that Calling-Based Commitment goes against everything our culture stands for. Yet confidence in such a counter-cultural stance is well-grounded because the Bible assures us that the basic concept of authority is for our good. After all, the most basic step of repentance we all take to become Christians recognizes that *the* absolute authority of the universe is unambiguously for our good. Every time authority is used well, it evidences that truth and becomes critical counterevidence to Satan's lie.

As such, it comes as no surprise that the writers of the New Testament Epistles see submission to authority—including the submission to love others in the local church—as integral to living out the gospel. Submission to authority is how we make "the best use of the time" in Ephesians (5:16; see 5:22–23; 6:1–4, 6–9). In Titus, it is how we make ourselves "ready for every good work" (3:1; see 2:3, 7, 9). And when Peter calls the church to "keep your conduct among the Gentiles honorable" (1 Pet. 2:12), his primary application—which covers much of the rest of the book—begins in the very next verse with the word *submit*.[8] Have you ever noticed how many different goals in the New Testament involve relating well to authority? Yes, calling people

---

[7] Letter from Lord Acton to Bishop Mandell Creighton, 1887.
[8] NIV

in your church to submit to the authority of church membership battles against their most basic assumptions as human beings. But the battle is worth fighting, because showing them the basic goodness of that authority is part of showing them God.

Now, putting this concept of Calling-Based Commitment into place involves a thousand details of church structure and operation, and those details are the topic of chapters 5–10. But before we turn there, we should examine another defining mark of Christian community in the New Testament.

4

Community
Goes Broad

My friend Bill Anderson first started visiting our church in his early 60s. He wasn't a Christian. At the time, he taught a popular class at Harvard University called "The Madness of Crowds," which teaches concepts of mass psychology by examining the phenomena of New England witch hunts, urban legends, and financial panics. But a career studying crowds did not prepare him for the local church. The diversity of the congregation impressed him. But beyond that, the *genuineness* of that diverse fellowship impressed him. In his words: "It was striking from the first moments I came through the door. It was clear that something special was going on. The relationships seemed not so much unnatural as highly uncommon. So I was introduced to the idea of a healthy church—a concept that had before eluded me." The power of this corporate witness provoked him. It undermined his conceptions of Christianity. And it began the process that would eventually lead to new life in Christ.

Where did this corporate witness come from? Well, when you became a Christian, you underwent a complete identity shift. Now, you *are* a new creation (2 Cor. 5:17); you *are* a child of God (Gal. 4:5); you *are* united to Christ (Rom. 6:1–8). Being a Christian is more fundamental to your identity than your family, your ethnicity, your profession, your nationality, your sexuality, your personality—or any other way this world defines identity. And so the unity you share with every Christian supersedes every other bond. That means that wherever gospel people exist, diversity should as well. Diversity grows naturally from the gospel.

As such, diversity is likely more important—and at the same time less important—than you've considered in the past. It's more important because, as Bill discovered, it is *the* grand witness to the truth of the gospel (Eph. 3:10). Far from "nice to have," diversity should be one of the most obviously supernatural characteristics of a local church. The visible bond of our unity shows off the power of an invisible gospel.

Yet at the same time, diversity may be less important than you've thought—because it is not an end in itself. Diversity is the effect, not the substance. The thermometer, so to speak, not the thermostat. It informs us of the spiritual temperature of our congregation, but has little ability to inflect maturity. Diversity in a local church matters very little in and of itself. It matters enormously to the extent that it advertises a deeper reality of gospel unity.

So why write a chapter about diversity if it's something that just "happens"? Because when we misunderstand the purpose and character of diversity in the local church, we often work *against* it. We build community based on similarity rather than the gospel. We are blind to the thousands of sacrifices we must make in order to love people who differ from us. In this chapter, we'll start by examining the *purpose* of diversity in Ephesians 3, then the *character* of diversity, and finally three common *impediments* to gospel unity in a local church.

The Purpose of Diversity

To get at the Bible's purpose for diversity in our churches, let's return to the book of Ephesians, which we examined in chapter 1. We'll start with Paul's purpose statement for the local church:

> To me, though I am the very least of all the saints, this grace was given, to preach to the Gentiles the unsearchable riches of Christ, and to bring to light for everyone what is the plan of the mystery hidden for ages in God who created all things, so that through the church the manifold wisdom of God might now be made known to the rulers and authorities in the heavenly places. This was according to the eternal purpose that he has realized in Christ Jesus our Lord. (Eph. 3:8–11)

What is God's *eternal* purpose? For the church to display his wisdom to all creation. How can we accomplish that? The specific characteristic Paul has in mind here is a "mystery"—hidden for ages in God who created all things. What is this mystery? He's already told us, in chapter 3, verse 6:

> This mystery is that the Gentiles are fellow heirs, members of the same body, and partakers of the promise in Christ Jesus through the gospel.

What God has done is amazing! For hundreds of years, God had promised that someday he would fold the Gentiles into his family. "It is too light a thing that you should be my servant to raise up the tribes of Jacob and to bring back the preserved of Israel; I will make you as a light for the nations, that my salvation may reach to the end of the earth" (Isa. 49:6). Now, in Christ, through Paul, God has kept this promise. Now, in Christ, the descendants of Abraham are not merely those who have his *flesh* but those who share his *faith*.

What is it about unity in God's family that makes even the "rulers and authorities in the heavenly places" take notice? It is the degree of separation between Jew and Gentile before Christ—a separation that Paul in Ephesians 2:14 calls a "dividing wall of hostility." It's not simply that these two groups were of different ethnicity (though they were), or that they were culturally distinct (though they were), or that for theological reasons they were kept apart (though they were)—it is that all of this separation was openly hostile. And yet in one moment, as Christ utters his last breath and the curtain separating man from God tears from top to bottom, he destroys the barrier dividing Jew from Gentile. Because of the extremity of their prior separation, God gets glory in their unity.

"But," a first-century reader might object, "that kind of unity is impossible! That would take a miracle!"

Precisely. Notice the connection between this unity and the prayer Paul concludes this section with in verses 14–19:

> For this reason I bow my knees before the Father, from whom every family in heaven and on earth is named, that according to the riches of his glory he may grant you to be strengthened with power through his Spirit in your inner being, so that Christ may dwell in your hearts through faith—that you, being rooted and grounded in love, may have strength to comprehend with all the saints what is the breadth and length and height and depth, and to know the love of Christ that surpasses knowledge, that you may be filled with all the fullness of God.

In the first part of Ephesians 3, Paul described the humanly impossible. So he concludes this section with a prayer for the impossible. He addresses the *Father*, praying for our strengthening with power through his *Spirit*, that we would know the vast dimensions of the love of *Christ* for us. His love is what powers our love. Together, all three persons of the Trinity accomplish his eternal purposes in the local church. And so Paul closes fittingly with his well-known doxology of verses 20–21:

> Now to him who is able to do far more abundantly than all that we ask or think, according to the power at work within us, to him be glory in the church and in Christ Jesus throughout all generations, forever and ever. Amen.

Paul asks for the impossible. But if God's power is "at work within us," God will do it, and so he will gain fame.

And that's true of your own church as well! As people with little in common in the world's eyes love each other as if they are closer than family, all heaven looks on with wonder at what the gospel has created.

So what is the "eternal purpose" of diversity in your own local church? To show off the power of the cross. And as we see in Ephesians 3, God's glory in our unity stems from the extremity of our prior separation. The analogy to marriage helps here: the paradox of Genesis 2 is that marriage celebrates diversity and unity simultaneously. The power of marriage is that husband and wife are different from each other. Eve was created as a helper who "corresponded to" or was "fit for" Adam (Gen. 2:18). And yet at the end of Genesis 2, we read that these two must "hold fast" to one another and be "one flesh" (v. 24). The strength of marriage lies in our differences from each other—but those differences are only weakness if there is no union, no oneness, no unity.

The analogy holds true in the local church. Our strength—our ability to showcase supernatural gospel power—is our diversity. And yet without unity that diversity is merely context for discord that defames the name of Christ.

So what kind of diversity proclaims the cross today?

What Diversity Matters?

Many reading this book live in places where churches share guilt for the moral scourge of racism. As a result, we care deeply about the presence of ethnic diversity in our churches. And this concern is noble. Scripture celebrates ethnic diversity. Certainly, that's at least part of what Paul speaks of in Ephesians 3.

But if by *diversity* we only ever mean *ethnic diversity*, we're missing the main message of Ephesians 3. After all, not every region of the world has ethnic diversity. The diversity I'm writing about is any multiplicity of backgrounds where unity is possible only through the gospel. With this as our standard, many types of differences fit the basic pattern of Ephesians 3. Think of all the different boundaries— respected by society—that the local church must transgress.

Boundaries of age. "Multigenerational" has become a buzzword among evangelicals for good reason: it's not something we often see in the world. This was perhaps the first kind of diversity that attracted me to my own church, as the generation who joined in the 1940s was infiltrated in the 1990s by a generation recently come of age. Amazingly, they functioned as a single community! Young men spent their Friday nights in nursing homes. Octogenarians vacationed in Cancun with twenty-somethings.

Boundaries of economics. Our world is familiar with rich people doing kind things for poor people. But then those rich people retreat to the comfort of other rich people—or at least those with a similar educational pedigree. Not so in the church. That's why James castigates the church's preferential treatment of the rich in James 2:8–9: "If you really fulfill the royal law according to the Scripture, 'You shall love your neighbor as yourself,' you are doing well. But if you show partiality, you are committing sin and are convicted by the law as transgressors."

Boundaries of politics. The local church must speak strongly on moral issues. But rarely does that moral authority translate cleanly into the details of public policy. As a result, Christians with divergent views on government policy should find unity in the more ultimate reality of God's kingdom. Of course, there are groups—such as the Nazi party in 1930s Germany—whose claim of moral authority so stretches credulity that the church must chose political sides. But by God's grace, we often find ourselves in less extreme situations.

Boundaries of social ability. Do socially awkward people describe your church as a refuge? Or do they find it as cold and impersonal as the world outside? Social ability is no barrier to true fellowship in the Spirit.

Boundaries of cultural background. Especially for those who grew up in the church, cultural background carries with it expectations for how a church should feel. As a result, some degree of sacrifice is necessary to have a church composed of Christians from suburban, rural, and urban backgrounds; liturgical, Pentecostal, and African-American religious traditions; and many different countries of origin. That's just fine. But explain to your congregation that everyone must sacrifice, in both the majority and the minority culture. Unity will often require sacrificing our interests for those of our brothers and sisters in the Lord.

If we seek boundary-crossing love that perplexes the world around us, then some types of diversity will often speak louder than others. A church in the suburbs of Boston comes to mind. Everyone might have similar skin color, but the congregation sits at the intersection of four towns with dramatically different class identities. So when a former addict from Weymouth spends nights and weekends speaking truth into the marriage of a Hingham banking executive, something is happening that perplexes the surrounding world. In my church, on the other hand, located in what has been one of the most ethnically segregated cities in the country, ethnic diversity speaks volumes. To be sure, ethnic diversity can be found among non-Christians in my city—so long as we're only talking about, for example, young political liberals from Ivy League schools. But the first comments I often hear from visitors is about how my church includes such dramatically different backgrounds—and yet still functions as a single community.

What about for your church? What boundaries has the gospel overrun that society fiercely respects?

Diversity (Should Be) Inevitable

This may all sound great—but how can we see this happen in our own churches? Local churches are not generally hallmarks of diversity. What's it going to take to change that?

My answer might at first sound naive, and even offensively naive. What must we do to create unity and diversity in our own churches? Nothing.

God has already done it. In a few paragraphs, I'll talk about how we must work hard to live it out. But consider for a moment how God has already created both unity and diversity in the gospel. Take the evidence of Ephesians 2–3 that I referenced a few pages back. I wonder if you've ever looked at the verbs Paul uses in this section of Scripture. Words like "separated," "alienated," "having no hope" of 2:12 and "been brought near," "is our peace," "has made us one," and "has broken down" in 2:13–14 are typical in the section on unity that stretches from 2:11 to the end of chapter 3. Every single verb is descriptive. This is no aspirational language; Paul simply describes what *has happened* in our salvation. From the beginning of Ephesians 2 to the end of Ephesians 3 there is just one imperative verb. Ephesians 2:11–12 tells us to "remember." "*Remember* that you were at that time separated from Christ, alienated from the commonwealth of Israel and strangers to the covenants of promise, having no hope and without God in the world" (v. 12). We must *remember* what we were so that we may fully understand what Christ has now done. That is all Paul tells us to do.

Of course, we must define exactly what type of unity Jesus's death has accomplished. It is not unity between all who *call* themselves Christians; it is unity between true Christians. And it is not organizational unity—as if we must all belong to the same denomination or family of churches. Nonetheless, we must recognize that this unity is an accomplished fact, and the bond we feel with true believers we have never met is testimony to it.

As heat radiates inevitably from a fire, unity in diversity flows inexorably from the gospel of Jesus Christ. There is nothing for us to *do* here; our role is merely to watch. And then to worship as God does the impossible in the community of the local church.

But does this mean we should lazily sit back and expect people with all different personalities and backgrounds to love each other automatically? Not at all. In fact, shortly after Paul establishes that it's God alone who unites Jew and Gentile in the Ephesian church, he tells them in Ephesians 4:3 to "maintain the unity of the Spirit in the bond of peace." As in so many of Paul's letters, the first half of Ephesians says, in effect, "This is who you are in Christ. You're not only sinners made alive, you're strangers made one." Then the second half of the book essentially says, "Therefore, live as who you are in Christ."

We have a role to play in cultivating unity. Like a farmer carefully watering a plant, we recognize that we're not the ones who give the plant of our unity its life. Yet we also recognize that in God's providence, what we do matters tremendously to keeping it healthy.

Too often, instead of celebrating unity in Christ, we actually get in the way—*resisting* the natural unity of the gospel. How do we do that? Much could be said, but let me close this chapter by looking at three impediments we throw up against unity and diversity.

Impediment 1
Ministry by Similarity

Speaking of farming, I'm not much of a gardener. But the past few years, I've been trying my hand at growing a variety of fruits and vegetables on our back deck—which (not having a yard)—functions simultaneously as playground, outdoor dining space, swimming pool, and family farm. My first year growing tomatoes, I watered them daily and planted them in well-drained pots. But then when the fruit ripened, I discovered with dismay plants full of rotten tomatoes. Searching furiously online, I discovered my problem: my overeager watering had flushed calcium out of the soil, leaving my plants malnourished. If I had had more faith in their ability to thrive under the hot summer sun, my summer harvest would have been more plentiful. Fortunately, some online advice saved the rest of the crop, though my wife gave me some hard stares when she saw me emptying calcium-based antacid tablets into the tomato pots.

My problem was not lack of action but lack of belief. And the same holds true in how we cultivate community in the local church. Paul describes unity and diversity not as a goal to achieve but as inexorable fact, a reality that exists wherever the gospel is at work. But we don't believe that the gospel can actually unite such a broad diversity of Christians. So instead, we take what feels like an easier path to community: we clump people based on similarity. Age-based groupings, marital-status-based groupings, profession-based group-ings, style-of-music-based groupings, etc. When we do this, we cer-tainly create a kind of community—that is, people living life together and enjoying fellowship together. But this community hardly pro-vokes the world's attention because the bond beneath it is natural similarity rather than the gospel.

If you take a bunch of twenty-something Yankees fans and stick them in a room together, they'll have a great time. They'll form great community. But you'll see the same thing happen whether or not these people are Christians. Think of all the ways we do ministry by similarity in our churches:

- Age-graded Sunday school classes. An extremely common prac-tice in my own Southern Baptist denomination.
- Small groups based on life stage. A small group for singles, for the newly married, for young families, for empty nesters, and so on.
- Support groups for various life-stage needs. Groups for divor-cees, for couples with kids in college, for medical professionals, accountants, families of alcoholics, and so forth.
- Men's ministries and women's ministries that are often further subdivided by age or family status.
- Groups limited to single adults.
- Entire churches aimed at specific homogeneous groups, like white-collar professionals or artists or homeschooling families.

I could go on. Ministry by similarity is a common tool for fostering community in churches. And too often, it stems from a lack of belief. We read how the gospel united Jew and Gentile in Ephesus, but we don't really see how it could unite single moms and retirees. And so we give each of them their own customized community.

At this juncture two facts about me will prove useful. (1) My wife and I have spent much of the last ten years leading small groups for newly married couples. (2) On behalf of the elders at my church, I help to oversee our women's ministry. So please don't misunderstand me. I don't believe that ministry by similarity is evil. It's just that I think it's dangerous. Ministry by similarity can so characterize our community as churches that it obscures the supernatural diversity that the gospel produces. Yet at the same time, I recognize the pastoral usefulness of relationships with people who share similarity.

What matters is what *characterizes* community in your church. The image of the "balanced food plate" used by the U. S. Department of Agriculture can be helpful here.[1] (When I was growing up it was the food pyramid, but apparently they've upgraded to a plate.) It's unhealthy to eat only burgers and fries; the plate has a section for fruits and vegetables, for grains, and for proteins. Similarly, we should cultivate a balanced plate of relationships in the church. There are relationships of similarity in the church—and we should be thankful for them. Relationships of similarity offer a level of understanding that is important and unique. But then—and this is key—there should also be relationships where you're *only* friends because you're Christians, without any worldly explanation. Both categories are healthy and important. Sometimes they overlap. But if that last category is nearly nonexistent, we should be concerned.

If you've constructed your community such that your visitors and members would describe most of it as affinity-based community, then you've undershot the vision of Ephesians 2 and 3.

Impediment 2
Consumerism

I've argued that unity amidst diversity is a natural outgrowth of the gospel. At first blush, this appeals to the consumerist mind-set that

---

[1] Credit for this analogy goes to my friend Matt Merker, who turned a draft of this chapter into a class on diversity for his church.

expects church to be "all about me." "I like the idea of going to a diverse church. And if diversity is something that just happens naturally, it shouldn't cost me anything!"

But Scripture overflows with descriptions of good things that grow naturally from the gospel—yet still require great sacrifice. "This is the will of God, your sanctification," Paul says in 1 Thessalonians 4:3. Yet despite the fact that sanctification is God's inviolable will, he goes on in the next verse to explain how each must "know how to control his own body." The fact that sanctification grows naturally from belief in the gospel in no way precludes a daily fight for holiness.

The same holds true for diversity. Yet in our consumerist age, we often assume it will happen without sacrifice. Take the simple question of what style of music we should use in our worship services. Many Christians approach the topic of music from a very individualistic perspective. "What kind of music will help me worship God the best?" But, of course, the diversity of our backgrounds—and especially our cultural backgrounds—mean that we'll have many different answers to that common question. Some churches have responded to this quandary by segmenting their church into multiple services or multiple locations based on musical style. Of course, this feeds right into the "ministry by similarity" that I just critiqued. Other churches—especially those with relative homogeneity—ignore the fact that their chosen musical style embodies any cultural overtones. Still others try to offer a grab bag of "something for everyone"—which requires both exquisite musicianship and a degree of sacrifice from everyone. And then there are churches that endeavor to make musical style as simple as possible so as to be accessible to as many types of people as possible—an approach I generally favor, but which requires its own degree of sacrifice.

And this is just musical style! There are similar challenges in nearly every other aspect of church life. But this is the whole point, isn't it? In his book, *Love in Hard Places*, Don Carson tells us, "Ideally

. . . the church itself is not made up of natural 'friends.' It is made up of natural enemies. What binds us together is not common education, common race, common income levels, common politics, common ancestry, common accents, common jobs, or anything else of that sort. . . . In this light, they are a band of natural enemies who love one another for Jesus' sake."[2] A church composed of natural friends says little about the power of the gospel. Yet the gospel-revealing community of natural enemies will require sacrifices in every aspect of our life together. Not surprisingly, when Paul in Romans 12:1 speaks those famed words, "present your bodies as a living sacrifice," his attention immediately moves in verse 4 to congregational life.

It's very possible to enjoy the idea of attending a diverse church, and yet never lift a finger to love someone who's quite different from you. So let's get practical. What kinds of sacrifices help foster unity in diversity?

- We can sacrifice our *comfort* to reach out and associate with someone whom we're not naturally drawn to. For a small example: when you see two different people you might talk to after a church service, make sure that at least half the time you walk up to the one you're less comfortable with.
- We can sacrifice our *preferences*: what kind of food we eat at the fellowship event; which songs we wish the church sang more often. Romans 12:10 says: "Love one another with brotherly affection."
- We can sacrifice our *resources and time* to serve fellow church members in need, even when society would deem their time less valuable than ours. First John 3:18 says: "Let us not love in word or talk but in deed and in truth." Consider the corporate lawyer billing a thousand dollars an hour, lingering patiently over lunch with her shopkeeper sister who (for the third time now) needs to hear the same advice.
- We can sacrifice our *habits* to spend time with those with whom we'd otherwise never see. If you're someone who always plans

---

[2] D. A. Carson, *Love in Hard Places* (Wheaton, IL: Crossway, 2002), 61.

your schedule two months out, spontaneously go to lunch after church with someone who's different from you.

Impediment 3
Invisibility of the Majority Culture

The first time someone said you spoke with an accent, you probably laughed it off. "I don't have an accent. It's *other* people who sound strange." The same holds true for a church culture. That culture may be striking to everyone on the outside, but invisible to those inside. Here's an example. The median age of my church is quite young (less than thirty)—and yet we have several dozen members in their sixties, seventies, and beyond. When I ask a young man in our congregation to lead in corporate prayer, his prayer often addresses what you might term "young man" concerns. Sexual purity, difficult bosses, challenging children, trying to make a difference in the world, etc. Now, in no way are those things foreign to the life of a church member in his seventies. But repeated prayers like that tell the seventy-year-old that this has become a "young person's church." Not just a church that's grown younger, but a church that's *for* young people. What about praying for trust in God when children have wandered from the faith? For strength to love when fatigue sets in? For wisdom to pass experience on to the next generation? The young man is not *trying* to make others feel excluded. But in a young church, his is the majority culture. And for the majority, culture is invisible. When the eighty-year-old leads our exceedingly young church in prayer, he more naturally prays about the concerns of the entire body.

When Paul in Romans 12:10–11 tells us to "love one another with brotherly affection" and to "outdo one another in showing honor," this must surely involve working to gain insight into the assumptions of my own culture so that I can care well for others. After all, how can you "bear one another's burdens" (Gal. 6:2) if you don't understand them?

I'll give you another example. As I write this, a verdict of "not guilty" has just been handed down in the murder trial of George

Zimmerman. Zimmerman was accused of racial bias in the shoot-
ing of an unarmed African-American youth. This event was hotly
debated in my city and elsewhere. Now, for many in my majority-
white church, this event did not seem to be a big deal. There was
even some confusion as to why it drew such widespread attention.
Yet for a substantial number of African-American members of my
congregation, this case was (and continues to be) profoundly dis-
turbing. The topic is one of racial profiling. And many of these dear
brothers and sisters have themselves been unfairly suspected, unfairly treated, or unfairly targeted because of the color of their skin.
The common reaction that I heard from this portion of my congregation was that the whole incident left them feeling much less safe
than they had felt before.

As a pastor, what should I do? I'm certainly not in a position to
opine on the correctness of the jury opinion. But if you think that the
most helpful response for my church is one of silence, you would be
mistaken. Silence would merely confirm the concern that, yes, our
church body has no idea what it is like to live in Washington, DC,
as an African-American. That, yes, I do in fact believe that everyone
in our church shares my own white, middle-class existence. Silence
would hardly be "outdoing one another in showing honor."

So in this case, our congregation prayed for all those left feeling
less safe because of this and other public incidents. That we would
understand each other, help each other, and ultimately put our hope
in a God who offers us perfect security in Christ. Rather than address
the case itself, we prayed about its impact—which is unmistakable,
significant, and largely hidden to many in our congregation.

Conclusion
How Do We Do This?
The community of the local church has supernatural breadth. This
diversity is not something we need to accomplish; it flows from the
accomplished work of Christ on the cross. Yet hard work remains if

we are to "maintain the unity of the Spirit in the bond of peace" (Eph. 4:3). For example, you may have noticed that while I noted three basic impediments to unity amidst diversity in the local church, I gave few suggestions for how to move past them. Just like I gave few ideas for nurturing supernatural *depth* of community in chapter 3. That's what the next section of this book seeks to accomplish.

Having articulated the problems in many evangelical churches, we'll now step through different aspects of congregational life—from prayer to preaching, from staffing to small groups. Over the next six chapters, my hope is to provide practical ideas for how your own congregation can better embody a biblical vision for community that is evidently supernatural.

Part 2

Fostering Community

5

Preach to Equip Your Community

Where does supernatural breadth and depth of community come from? How do we cultivate it?

The answer is simple. Supernatural community comes from supernatural faith, which comes from God's Word (see Rom. 10:17). Your church needs to hear God's Word.

But here's what you might miss. Your church needs more than the Sunday morning sermon. Nurturing the community I've described in these chapters requires saturating your people in God's Word. And that's not something you can do in a single sermon on Sunday morning. Your people need to hear God's Word all week long, from each other. But not all preaching equips them to do that.

This is not a chapter just on preaching. It's about the fact that preaching should create a congregation of minipreachers. It's not just about teaching; it's about equipping. It's about the kind of preaching that fuels the supernatural community we all want to see in our churches.

An Example
Cultivating a Culture of Discipling

Suppose you want to cultivate a culture of discipling in your church. That is, a culture where it's normal and expected for members to design their friendships to help each other follow Jesus. You want it to be commonplace for people to meet together one-on-one to study God's Word and encourage each other in Christ. But that's not yet typical of relationships in your church. What do you do? A few ideas come to mind:

- You could preach a series on discipling where you instruct your people on what to do.
- You could hire a pastor for discipling.
- You could launch a discipling campaign, where people pair up and work through a prescribed curriculum.
- You could exhort them extra hard next Sunday not just to read the Bible, but to live it.
- You could require discipling as one component of church membership.

Many of these may be legitimate courses of action. But they all focus on manufacturing right decisions right now. They don't necessarily change your underlying church culture, which involves people's assumptions about what it means to be a Christian. You don't merely want to start a few discipling relationships; you want people to see that loving others this way is part of following Jesus.

A chronic temptation for church leaders is to see a deficit in our churches and then "fix it," that is, adjust the behavior of our congregation to better reflect Scripture. But while many of our solutions may change behavior in the short-term, they do little to create real, long-lasting change. It's like parenting. As much as you want obedient, well-behaved kids, you know that heart change is much more important.

Real Change Comes from Faith

At its core, every problem in your congregation is a problem of unbelief. If you want to form a culture of discipling in your church, your people must believe Jesus's words. They must believe that "it is more blessed to give than to receive" (Acts 20:35). They must believe that they will grow best as they help others grow. They must believe that there is more joy in helping others than in an exclusive focus on their own spiritual health. The challenge of building a culture of discipling is a challenge of faith.

How can we give our congregations greater faith? We can't. Faith is always a gift from God (Eph. 2:8). Yet in his mercy, God has told us how he works. He creates faith by his Word: "Faith comes from hearing, and hearing through the word of Christ" (Rom. 10:17). The amazing thing about God's Word is that it doesn't merely tell us what to do; it can create what it commands. Think of Jesus speaking to a deaf man in Mark 7—thus creating his ability to hear. Or to a dead man in John 11—thus creating his ability to obey. To see your congregation grow in faith-filled action, saturate them with God's Word.

We Need More Than a Sermon

Fifteen years ago, my church faced the question of how to cultivate a culture of discipling. We realized that the problem was deeper than it appeared. It wasn't merely that people needed to form spiritually intentional relationships with each other. The problem was that they didn't see this as an implicit part of following Jesus. We needed a culture change, not just a behavior change. So what would have happened if we'd simply adopted the approaches I mentioned earlier? We would have done an excellent job of replicating one type of relationship across the congregation. But discipling should look different depending on who's doing it, right? One model won't fit everyone. After all, a "programmatic" approach to change wouldn't really adjust people's basic assumptions about the Christian life. It wouldn't address the underlying faith issue. A topical sermon series and new hire wouldn't necessarily be bad for our congregation—but they would only scratch the surface of the change we needed.

So what did we do? As you might suspect, we didn't make any new hires, launch a discipling campaign, or adjust our small group structure. Instead, we prayed about this need. And we continued preaching through God's Word. Knowing that the congregation struggled in this area, discipling showed up frequently in sermon application all over the Bible.

What happened? Bit by bit, God's Word began to travel. People began to see how the Bible's "one another" commands could be lived out—often in ways the elders hadn't even considered. They began talking with each other about their friendships in the church, using biblical categories to assess them. Friendships became more spiritually deliberate. Sunday school teachers talked about discipling in their classes. Small groups became hubs of discipling activity. Over time, discipling went from unusual to normal.

I hope you see how much more deeply rooted and complex this is than a congregation simply "doing what the pastor tells them." It took years, but over time, thousands of conversations about how to apply God's Word really did change our church culture. We taught them God's Word, and God's Spirit prompted them to continue repeating that Word to one another in ways we never would have thought of.

Here's an important question, then: in this example, how would you describe the Word ministry that created a culture of discipling? Was it a ministry of the pulpit? Well, it began there. But then it became the ministry of the congregation—through friendships, teachers, small groups, and others. That was the real agent of change.

The model comes from Ephesians 4: "[Christ] gave the apostles, the prophets, the evangelists, the shepherds and teachers, to equip the saints for the work of ministry, for building up the body of Christ" (vv. 11–12).

Christ gave the church ministers of the Word not to effect change, but to equip others to effect change. The Sunday morning sermon isn't the finish line for Word ministry, it's the starting line. It is the beginning of the real work, as your congregation takes God's Word and puts it to work through the week. To use another metaphor, the job of a sermon isn't to be a snowmaker that gives snow to the people. It is to start an avalanche—a chain reaction of God's Word. That is where real culture change comes from.

When addressing deficits in your church culture, your change management plan should begin with the word *preach*. Yet the ministry of the Word that will actually accomplish that change isn't mainly the Sunday morning sermon. It's not even people talking about the Sunday morning sermon. Instead, it is preaching that gives your people the tools to pick up that Word and become ministers themselves.

But therein lies the problem. Not all preaching equips the flock to become minipreachers. So not all preaching cultivates lasting culture change in a congregation. Sometimes that's because preaching has little connection to Scripture. To repeat an oft-used metaphor, preachers often use Scripture as a diving board—starting with the text but then quickly moving to their own ideas. Instead, we should think of Scripture as the swimming pool. But even among swimming-pool preachers, we often fail to preach in a way that equips our congregations.

- Some preaching spoon-feeds application without explaining the text. That makes it quite difficult for the congregation to become Word ministers to each other.
- Some preaching succeeds in explaining the text but fails to show the congregation how to understand the Scriptures when left to themselves.
- Some preaching tells the congregation what to do without understanding why it may be challenging for them to do it. That leaves them ill-equipped to apply Scripture to each other through the week.

What kind of preaching equips a congregation to become Word ministers themselves? First, your preaching must be responsive to your particular flock, no matter its size. You must understand them. Otherwise, they might as well download their favorite celebrity pastor's sermons off the Internet. Second, you must teach them their responsibility for the Word and equip them to use it. Let's turn our attention to these two challenges.

Understanding the Needs of Your Congregation

If your preaching is to equip your people, you must understand them. Part of this is obvious. For example, if you know that your congregation struggles with legalism, how well can you help them unless you understand how this sin surfaces in their lives?

But part of this is more subtle, involving the relationship between leadership, trust, and understanding. Leadership depends on trust, doesn't it? For example, let's say you have marriages in your congregation on the brink of divorce. Your congregation must understand that Christians don't simply divorce when human hope for a marriage dries up. But that message is so countercultural as to be offensive, isn't it? It can lead to a lot of fear. Fear, for example, that you just don't understand the difficulty of a particular marriage.

That fear presents a real barrier to your leadership. How will your congregation trust your authority instead of fearing it? Well, think about what God does in our relationship with him. Among other reasons to trust him in Psalm 103 is the comfort of verse 14: "For he knows our frame; he remembers that we are dust." God's not going to ask us to do something that will prove undoable. He *knows* us! Or to venture into the world of marriage, how can a husband help his wife not give way to fear (1 Pet. 3:6)? He can live with her in an understanding way (1 Pet. 3:7).

In any relationship of authority, the antidote to fear is understanding. We fear authority that's used without regard for our needs. But when one in authority shows he understands and has considered our situation and needs, trust becomes attractive.

A friend in Beijing was part of a congregation that was transitioning from a monocultural congregation to a multicultural congregation. Like others, this man resisted the change. No argument from Scripture could convince him to give up the comfort of a congregation of people just like him. But one day his pastor did something that changed everything. For a moment, he stopped speaking about why the change was biblical and talked instead of his love for this people. With great emotion, he explained how deeply he understood the difficulty of what he was asking. Suddenly, in the knowledge of that love and understanding, my friend considered the Scriptures with a new heart. And he became exactly the kind of Word minister that Paul writes of in Ephesians 4, encouraging others in this new direction. Truth alone could not equip him to become a minister of the Word; it was truth and love, expressed through understanding.

So how can we incorporate an understanding of our congregations into our preaching? Let me make three suggestions.

1. Don't Just Preach to Them; Pastor Them

To pastor is to shepherd. Yet a movement exists to specialize pastoral staff, giving one man responsibility merely for preaching and vision. Meanwhile, other pastors attend to the day-to-day needs of the congregation. This trend will not serve us well. Much of your ability to preach well comes from your understanding of your congregation. And much of your understanding of your congregation comes from the time you spend caring for them. For the pastor of a small congregation, this advice is beside the point. Who else would do this work? But for those with the freedom to delegate, refrain from delegating all pastoral work no matter the importance of time in your study and on the road.

Aside from that, the preacher-as-pastor model takes advantage of a wonderful synergy between preaching and shepherding. Your love as a shepherd augments your authority as a preacher. And your care as a preacher augments your authority as a shepherd. It's a virtuous cycle that builds trust. And trust is one of the most valuable commodities you will ever trade in as an undershepherd of Jesus Christ.

2. Involve Your Congregation in Writing Your Sermons

I'm not advocating "open source sermons," but I am suggesting something beyond a pastor disappearing for two days into his study and emerging with food for the flock. There are many ways to do this, and not all will work for your congregation. But here are three for your consideration:

Pray through the Passage Together. Our staff and elders open our staff meetings and elders meetings by reading through the passage for next Sunday and then take turns praising God for something we each see in the passage. It's a good way to start a meeting. But beyond that, I often hear how the passage touches people in ways I didn't expect. And that opens new thoughts as to how it can be applied.

Application Lunches. One useful way to construct sermon application is to brainstorm through predefined application categories for each point in the sermon.[1] If you do something like this, always make it a group project. In exchange for a free lunch, invite a few members of your church to spend time thinking and praying through the passage ahead of time. Then once your sermon points take shape, work together over lunch to generate application ideas for each point. The benefit is a sermon that addresses perspectives beyond your own.

Saturday Night Sermon Reading. Consider doing a "dry run" through the sermon on Saturday evening. Invite a few folks from the church to listen. You'll work out some communication bugs before Sunday morning. Beyond that, it's a great opportunity for people

---

[1] For more details on developing an "application grid," see the 9Marks book, *Preach*, by Mark Dever and Greg Gilbert (Nashville, TN: B&H, 2012), 93–94. They suggest brainstorming application in seven different categories for each sermon point. (1) How does the teaching in this point fit into the salvation-historical progression of the biblical story line? (2) What does this text say to the non-Christian? (3) What does it say to the larger society and to policy makers? (4) What does it say about Jesus? (5) How does it apply to the individual Christian? (6) Does it say anything in particular about issues of work or family? (7) What does it say to my own local church? In a three-point sermon, this would generate twenty-one separate application points. Obviously, you won't use all of them. But select the best of the lot and you'll have a good shot at useful application in your sermon.

to provide criticism *before* the sermon gets preached. And it's an opportunity to get feedback on areas you've not quite figured out—particularly regarding illustrations and the introduction.

3. Get Feedback on Your Sermons

Opportunities to speak to the needs and heart of your congregation often become apparent only after you've delivered a sermon. But that's no reason to lose these insights; you'll only preach better if you regularly submit your sermons to critique, week after week. After you preach, gather a group of members to analyze the morning sermon. So many pastors *say* that Scripture is their final authority for faith and practice—yet they never give opportunity for others to critique them against the standards of those same Scriptures. I think that suggests unwarranted confidence in our judgment.

Preaching is a two-way conversation, even though only half of that conversation is visible to the congregation. You're well aware of how facial expressions, body posture, and verbal feedback of the hearers affect how you deliver your message. A sermon review enhances that second half of the conversation. What was clear? What was confusing? What opportunities for application did you miss? What might have come across as inconsiderate? What did people appreciate? Make sure to invite those who have likely had conversations with others after the sermon. That way a small group of members can represent a broad cross-section of the congregation.

If you want preaching that equips, you must *understand* your people. Beyond that, however, equipping-focused preaching teaches your people to use God's Word themselves. Let's turn now to that second challenge.

Preach to Help Your People Use God's Word

Many people think that your responsibility is to preach a sermon and their responsibility is to listen and apply it to their lives. That vastly underestimates the responsibility of a sermon listener. Think back to that section of Ephesians 4 that I referenced earlier in the chapter. You equip the saints through the preaching of God's Word. And then they use God's Word to minister to each other. That certainly starts with listening and with personal application—and yet it is much, much more. In a Word-saturated congregation, a sermon doesn't stop when it reaches the ears of your people. Instead, it continues its ministry through them day after day, all through the week. In his book, *Reverberation*, Jonathan Leeman puts it well:

> The problem . . . is that God's Word is not always massaged through the life of the congregation, like yeast through dough. People show up on Sunday for the sermon, and often do little more. The ministry of the Word stops at noon.
>
> The "ministry of the Word" indeed *begins* in the pulpit, but then it must *continue* through the life of the church as members echo God's Word back and forth to one another. The word reverberates, as in an echo chamber. In a real echo chamber, sound reverberates off the walls. In the church, it's the hearts of people that both absorb and project the sounds of His effectual Word.[2]

How do we engender this response to God's Word in our congregations? How can we preach God's Word in such a way that God's people become ministers of that same Word? Let me submit three ideas for your consideration.

1. Clarify the Congregation's Responsibility for Preaching

Teach your congregation their responsibility for the preaching they hear. Specifically, they have responsibility in three areas:

- Responsibility for what preaching they support. In Galatians 1 and 2 Timothy 4:3, Paul admonishes the *congregation* for the

---

[2] Jonathan Leeman, *Reverberation* (Chicago: Moody, 2011), 24. If you want to grow more confidence in God's Word—and a better appreciation of how his Word can change your church from the inside out—I would highly commend Jonathan's short book. It describes the life-giving ministry of God's Word as it reverberates from the sermon into the day-to-day life of your people.

preaching they listen to rather than simply addressing their teachers. Similarly, when the church at Pergamum tolerates the teaching of Balaam and the Nicolaitans, the Spirit addresses the *churches* (Rev. 2:17).

- Responsibility to change. James 1:22 reminds us that we are not merely to be hearers of the Word, but doers of the Word. Similarly, according to Luke 12:48, every good word we hear increases our responsibility before God.
- Responsibility to help each other change. Your people must understand that preaching is a corporate activity, not an individual one. Change comes when the congregation uses preaching to minister to each other, as Paul writes in Ephesians 4. To paraphrase my earlier quote from Leeman, preaching that equips is not simply truth that we hear on Sunday, but truth that reverberates back and forth through the congregation all week long.

2. Equip Your People to Better Read the Scriptures

Has anyone ever told you after a sermon, "Wow! I could never have gotten that myself!" People mean that as a compliment. But often it's a sign of failure. Your preaching should equip the congregation to become ministers of the Word themselves. It should show them how to mine the Scriptures for insight when you're not around. Here are some thoughts on doing that:

- Preach expositional sermons. Sometimes a topical sermon or series can be helpful. But mainly, each sermon should simply explain and apply a text of Scripture. That way, the point of the text becomes the point of your sermon. If most of your preaching consists of sermons like "Five Biblical Imperatives for Parents," you'll never get beyond simply telling your people what to do. But if most of your preaching is expositional, you will teach your people how to *use* the Scriptures. As people listen to a steady diet of your preaching, do they become less dependent on you to understand and apply the Bible?

- Preach to teach context. For many, the primary challenge in understanding and using the Bible is determining how a passage emerges from its context. So when you preach, show your contextual work. Let's say you're preaching 1 Corinthians 13 on love. Rather than simply applying the amazing truth that Paul has in this passage, show them how the passage fits together, how the logic flows from verse 1 to verse 13. Then show them how the passage fits into the argument of 1 Corinthians: how each item Paul describes is something the Corinthians lack. And then, finally, show them the role that this chapter plays in fitting the whole Bible together: how the goal of our salvation isn't simply escape from hell, but a community of supernatural love.

- Preach from observation. The best tool for understanding Scripture is not a commentary or a seminary degree; it is observation. Thankfully, this is a tool available to every Christian. Your preaching should demonstrate the power of observation. Don't simply answer difficult questions in the text; show how clues in the surrounding verses clarify the answer. I hope that your congregation responds to your sermons by saying, "Wow! That's insightful! But I can see that if I'd spent a few hours staring at that text, I'd have seen most of that as well."

- Encourage your church to study the text during the week. If you advertise in advance what text you'll preach on next, people can read and study it ahead of time. Then they can engage with the text while you preach rather than simply sitting back while you spoon-feed sermon application.

3. Provide Sermon Application That Is Corporate and Collaborative

The Bible is mainly addressed to God's people collectively: the community of faith. Is your sermon application similarly corporate in nature? Here are some ideas if it's not:

- Suggest as sermon application conversations that members might have—perhaps over lunch after the morning service.

"Later on today, be sure to ask someone in our congregation ways in which they've received grace upon grace from Jesus Christ (John 1:16)." Or, "At your lunch table today, have everyone share one lie they're tempted to believe about conflict (James 4:1)." At the very least, this practice can help kill the satanic culture of church people talking about absolutely anything after the service *except* for the sermon.

- As sermon application, suggest how your congregation can pray for your church. For example, that we would believe the trust-worthiness of Scripture (Isa. 40:8), or that as a body we would be faithful to tell each other's children about the goodness of God (Judg. 2:10).

- Provide application for your congregation as a whole. For example, "One implication of 3 John 6 is that we should be generous with the missionaries we're supporting as a church." Or, "If Hebrews 3:13 tells us to 'exhort one another every day' about God's promises and faithfulness, it should be normal in our conversations together to encourage each other with Scripture."

Let's preach sermons that equip our congregations to become the primary ministers of the Word in our churches.

Preaching to Ongoing Controversy in Your Church

Normally, preaching to equip your people happens in a somewhat generic way. You give them the tool of Scripture, not knowing exactly what issues and challenges you're preparing them for. But sometimes, especially when a church is facing controversy and division, your preaching must equip the flock to address a specific challenge. And this requires careful, prayerful judgment. It balances the need to protect the flock from wolves (Matt. 7:15) with the need to protect congregational unity (Eph. 4:3). Here is some advice in doing this well, geared specifically for the main preacher in your congregation.

Be patient. Especially early on in your ministry, countless opportunities arise to tackle issues head-on in preaching that would divide your congregation and/or get you fired. In general, you can accomplish more gospel good over your lifetime if you patiently bear with a congregation instead of confronting an issue head-on. Through patience, you allow the Spirit to do his work through his Word. Mark 4:26–27 is a great encouragement in this regard: "The kingdom of God is as if a man should scatter seed on the ground. He sleeps and rises night and day, and the seed sprouts and grows; he knows not how."

God's Word is living and active, even when you are not. Be patient and watch it take root and flourish.

Only with reluctance should you address disputable issues. First Corinthians 15:3–4 is a good summary of what is core to the gospel message: "For I delivered to you as of first importance what I also received: that Christ died for our sins in accordance with the Scriptures, that he was buried, that he was raised on the third day in accordance with the Scriptures." The further an issue is from these foundational truths, the less likely it would be wise for you to confront it directly in your sermon.

When possible, speak with people individually rather than through a sermon. It's tempting to address an issue in the Sunday sermon rather than risk an awkward private conversation. If Rob and Rachel are gossiping, don't merely attack "gossiping" in your sermon and hope they will listen. Talk with Rob and with Rachel.

Give people principles and let them work out the implications. I'm amazed at how often, when provided with biblical principles, people can come to the right answer by themselves without my having to tell them explicitly. Let's say, for example, that your missions budget is cluttered with support for subpar work by missionaries your congregation doesn't know anymore. And that's keeping you from supporting a fantastic missions candidate your congregation is looking to send out. Simply teach your congregation about supporting missionaries well (3 John 6) and the importance of making strategic investments in missions work (1 Cor. 3:10–15). Don't tell your congregation explicitly what changes to make in the budget—at least not at first. Having seen those principles in Scripture, many in your congregation will do the math themselves. Then some of them will start pushing in the right direction. If eventually you do need to provide explicit direction for the budget, momentum will be behind you.

Conclusion
A Second Ingredient

Community with supernatural breadth and depth can only come through supernatural faith. This chapter has focused on one ingredient of real, God-given faith: God's Word. But of course, prayer is another. And so it is to that topic that we'll now turn.

6

Pray Together as
a Community

The Power of Prayer: The New York Revival of 1858 by Samuel Prime is
one of the most captivating yet repetitive books you will ever read.[1]
On the one hand, the story will captivate your imagination. In 1857,
the Old North Dutch Reformed Church on Fulton Street in Manhattan was struggling. So they employed Jeremiah Lanphier as a missionary to the neighborhood. Overwhelmed at his task, Lanphier
asked, "Lord, what wilt thou have me do?"

God gave no audible answer to his prayer, and lacking any better
ideas, Lanphier advertised a lunchtime prayer meeting at the church.
For the first twenty minutes, he prayed by himself. By the end of the
hour, six others had joined him. The next week twenty gathered for
prayer; the next week thirty. Soon the building was filled, and additional churches and even theaters became prayer meeting sites. The
Herald Tribune noted the flood of businessmen streaming to churches
across the city at lunchtime and began publishing a series of stories
about the remarkable meetings. Within six months, fifty thousand
met daily for prayer in Manhattan, with similar meetings sprouting

---

[1] Samuel Prime, *The Power of Prayer* (1859; repr., Edinburgh: The Banner of Truth Trust, 2009).

up in Philadelphia, Baltimore, Washington, DC, Richmond, Savannah, and elsewhere.

Yet the book is repetitive. It is little more than Prime's simple notation of prayers made and responses given. A wife prays for her husband; he turns up at the next day's meeting, converted. A man prays for his son who at that moment is finding salvation in a different city. An Irish Catholic attends, is convicted of his sins, and comes to faith in Christ. He asks for prayer for his wife, who is similarly converted. A mother asks for prayer for her two distant children; they are drawn that very night to a church where they both come to know Christ. A man on the verge of murder and suicide visits a meeting, is saved, and changed. The style of the book is anything but gripping. Prime records no emotional appeals or sensational preaching. At the ring of a bell at noon, a hymn would be sung, requests given, and prayers made. The meetings adjourned precisely at 1 p.m.

That steady cadence of prayers made, prayers answered, prayers made, prayers answered in the book is striking. Repetition that might otherwise bore you to tears instead draws you to the very throne room of heaven in amazement at God's astounding faithfulness. There is no "secret" to prayer laid out in this book. Instead, one of the greatest movements of prayer in modern history was ordinary to the extreme. And through it God acted with extraordinary power: two years before a bloody civil war began, as many as a million Americans were converted through what became known later as the "Layman's Prayer Revival."[2]

Prayer is an ordinary means to accomplish supernatural ends. So as ordinary people seeking to cultivate supernatural community, how can we ignore prayer? Yet here we find a strange disconnect.

On the one hand, we evangelicals understand the importance of prayer. We pray in our churches, in our quiet times, at the dinner table, even in the car. We buy books on prayer, hear sermons on prayer, go to seminars on prayer, and sign up for prayer chains.

---

[2] John Hannah, "The Layman's Prayer Revival of 1858," *Bibliotheca Sacra* 134 (January 1977): 533.

But can you think of anything that's as important, yet less prayed for, than the local church? On the one hand, the supernatural community of the local church is the focal point of God's redemptive plan to make the nations his inheritance. And that supernatural work is entirely outside of our control. Sounds like the perfect recipe for fervent prayer, doesn't it? But how often does the average evangelical pray for God to do this work in his local church? How much time do *you* spend praying for *your* church?

That is the topic of this chapter. But don't expect to find some transformative secret buried in these pages. I started this chapter with Samuel Prime's account because I want you to grasp the power of ordinary prayer. Further, because prayer *for* the church begins with prayer *as* the church, the ordinary prayer I'll spend most of this chapter discussing is corporate prayer. We'll begin by exploring the importance of corporate prayer for the local church. Then we'll get practical, looking at what we should pray for together and how we should pray. Finally, we'll finish with some implications for Christians when they pray for the church on their own.

The Importance of Corporate Prayer for Church Life

It's interesting: reading the Bible cover to cover, you pass hundreds of pages without any reference to corporate prayer. In fact, there are almost no examples of corporate prayer in the entire Old Testament.[3] Even the Psalms, intended for temple worship, generally speak in the first person singular. Prayer in the Old Testament is nearly always through a human mediator.

But when Jesus teaches his disciples to pray in Matthew 6:11–12, his prayer is corporate: "Give *us* this day *our* daily bread, and forgive *us our* debts as *we* also have forgiven *our* debtors." So with the arrival of the church in the book of Acts, corporate prayer explodes onto

---

[3] The clearest examples are phrase-long prayers in Judges 10:10 and 1 Samuel 12:10 or the prayer in Nehemiah 9. Most well-known prayers in the Old Testament—like Daniel 9 or 1 Chronicles 6—are prayed by just one man.

the scene. The disciples pray together to find Judas's replacement in Acts 1. The new church devotes itself to prayer in Acts 2. They gather in Acts 4 to praise God for Peter and John's release from the rulers and elders of Jerusalem. In Acts 8, the disciples pray together for the Spirit to fall on the Samaritans. In Acts 12 the church prays together for Peter's rescue from Herod. In Acts 13 the church at Antioch prays together to commission Saul and Barnabas. And later, as he writes to the Corinthians, Paul assumes that their meetings together regularly include corporate prayer (1 Cor. 11:4; 14:15).

Corporate prayer has an impressive New Testament pedigree, and for that reason alone it should rate as a significant piece of church life. Yet in so many of our churches, corporate prayer takes a distant back seat to music and the sermon. Imagine that! In church, we gather to see God build something that is evidently supernatural. But other than a short prayer of invocation at the beginning of the service and before the sermon, we spend little time together in prayer.

Here are some reasons to spend significant time in corporate prayer—which I hope will help you better articulate its value for your own local church.

Corporate Prayer Is How We Publicly Ask God to Act

Paul tells the Corinthian church, "You also must help us by prayer, so that many will give thanks on our behalf for the blessing granted us through the prayers of many" (2 Cor. 1:11). Public prayer results in public praise when God answers. And God's overriding concern through all of history is that his glory be known publicly. "For the earth will be filled with the knowledge of the glory of the LORD as the waters cover the sea" (Hab. 2:14).

To illustrate, put yourself in the shoes of a pastor friend of mine. He was leading a youth group trip when a loud *CRACK* from the bottom of their ancient bus interrupted the drive, a thousand miles from home. Upon further inspection, the problem became clear: the drive shaft had split in two. And now my friend faced a dilemma. Would he gather the teenagers around him to pray for God to fix the bus? What if God didn't provide? How would he explain that to the kids? After all, it wasn't like the problem was simply a flat tire. The *drive shaft* was broken.

Well, he did lead in prayer. After all, he figured, God is fully capable of protecting his own reputation. He doesn't need us to hedge his bets for him. And, as you can imagine in this happy story, a friendly mechanic appeared who happened to know of a scrap yard nearby that happened to have a spare drive shaft on hand. He towed the bus in, welded the new drive shaft in place, and the bus was off and running.

God loves to defend his reputation. When we pray together, our needs become public. When he answers, his glory becomes public.

Corporate Prayer Teaches Our People How to Pray

If biblical community is to take shape in your church, your people must pray. But I think my church is typical in that, left to ourselves, we pray most fervently about relatively trivial things. For a car to be fixed or a test to be passed or a cold to be healed, for example. It's good to pray for these trivial matters. But how pathetic when they dominate our prayers! How can we teach our people to really pray? How can we lift their focus out of their own circumstances to join God's grand purposes for this world? I can think of little that could be better than modeling prayer, week in and week out, as we pray together. By praying corporately, we emphasize spiritual priorities over physical circumstances. And we emphasize our life together corporately over our needs as individuals.

Corporate Prayer Is a Collective Experience

As we pray to our heavenly Father "from whom every family in heaven and on earth is named" (Eph. 3:15), we remember where true unity comes from. In God's larger purposes, we find our hearts drawn together. God has given us corporate prayer as a wonderful tool to foster unity. Why would we ever lay it aside?

To summarize, what about corporate prayer makes it important? The public nature of corporate prayer serves God's desire to make his glory known. The didactic nature of corporate prayer teaches our people how they should pray. And the communal nature of corporate prayer builds unity through a shared voice to God.

What Should We Pray about Corporately?

Now, if corporate prayer is this important, we should be deliberate in what we pray about. Perhaps you've heard the acronym ACTS (adoration, confession, thanksgiving, supplication) suggested as a model for personal prayer. ACTS also serves as a good outline for corporate prayer. So with the goal of deliberately shaping our corporate prayer, I'll walk through each of these four. In doing so, I'll share some principles my own congregation has found useful.

Prayers of Adoration

In my experience, we evangelicals more easily thank God for things he's done than praise him for who he is. Thanksgiving, while important, is about God's treatment of *us*. Praise is pure response to the magnificence of *him*. As a result, a dedicated time to praise God in prayer (without straying into thanksgiving) offers real benefit to your congregation. For example, instead of a prayer thanking God for rescuing us from our sin, a prayer of praise would praise God for the enormity of his mercy. Consider two, three, or even ten minutes of corporate prayer each week focused purely on praise.

Prayers of Confession

Similar to our difficulty with praising God, we can often become squeamish about spending sustained time in confession. Many times, our "prayers of confession" turn into part confession, part petition for God's forgiveness, and part thanksgiving for our forgiveness in Christ. Of course, this petition and thanksgiving absolutely has a place in our services. But a worthy goal for your public services is to dedicate several minutes to consider the heinousness of our offenses before God. Only after holding ourselves "under the water" for several minutes will the good news of the gospel ring with the joy that it should.

Prayers of Thanks

Thanksgiving advertises that there is nothing we have that we did not receive from above (1 Cor. 4:7). It roots our concern for the future in God's faithfulness in the past. Most commonly, churches offer a prayer of thanks before collecting an offering from the congregation. This presents a wonderful opportunity to express thanks for God's financial blessing. Beyond that, we can use that time to thank him for so much else, of which the money in the offering plate is but a shadow and token.

Prayers of Supplication

We're good at asking God for things, aren't we? Yet how well do our requests reflect God's desires for us? As fallen creatures, we default to prayer for physical circumstances instead of requests with more spiritual aims. What you pray publicly will guide how your people pray privately. So take care in how you shape those requests.

Part of shaping these requests is explaining *why* we ask God for things. Consider opening your corporate prayers of petition with Daniel's prayer in Daniel 9.

> O my God, incline your ear and hear. . . . We do not present our pleas before you because of our righteousness, but because of your great mercy. O Lord, hear; O Lord, forgive. O Lord, pay attention and act. Delay not, for your own sake, O my God, because your city and your people are called by your name." (vv. 18–19)

We don't ask God for things because we deserve them. In fact, with all that he has given us in Christ, it is almost embarrassing to go to him, asking for more. But we ask because he tells us to. We ask for *his* sake: we are called by his name, and what happens to us reflects on him. We want him to get all the glory when he answers our prayers.

In addition to modeling *why* we ask, we can model *what* to ask. Here are three ideas for structuring what your church asks for corporately.

1. Pray through a Reasonably Comprehensive List of Biblical Priorities

As an example, here is what one of my church's elders leads the congregation in prayer for each Sunday morning in our "prayer of petition."

- Pray for physical needs within your congregation. Even though your church may face more pressing concerns, it's important to show that physical needs are worthy of prayer.
- Pray for specific individuals in your congregation. Sometimes the reasons you pick these people are clear; sometimes you simply pick them at random. Both are helpful. It reminds a congregation of their responsibility for each of their brothers and sisters.
- Pray for other evangelical churches in your area. This has the wonderful effect of showing the unity and partnership we enjoy with them in the gospel.
- Pray with respect for those in authority, as 1 Timothy 2:2 instructs us. This might be government at a national or local level—or people like school teachers or media CEOs who steward less formal authority over us.
- Pray for issues facing your city or region, such as joblessness, drought, or corruption. Pray that God would allow justice to prevail and mercy to prosper. And pray that God would use temporary deprivation to lead people to eternal security through the gospel.
- Pray for leaders of different foreign governments, that they would rule wisely and understand the common grace of religious

freedom. And pray for church planting in these countries. Books like *Operation World* can inform these prayers.

- Pray for missionaries your church supports.
- Pray for the persecuted church and for the gospel to go forth even in difficult situations.
- Finally, turning your attention back to your own congregation, pray through the points of the sermon you're about to preach. Ask God to change your people by his Spirit as you explain his Word to them.

2. Develop a List of the Things You Hope Will Increasingly Characterize Your Church

As a sample, here's a list of eleven elements of our church culture I developed for my church several years ago. We pray through two or three of these each week as part of our Sunday evening prayer meeting.

- Pray for our witness of unity in diversity.
- Pray for our daily lives this week at work and at home. Pray that we would do what is good, honor God, and commend the gospel.
- Pray that we would see relationships in the local church as part of what it means to be a Christian.
- Pray that we would understand the need to make our relationships at church transparent, to be willing to tell embarrassing things about ourselves and to ask awkward questions when needed.
- Pray that we would expect conversations with other church members to be deep, and often theological in nature.
- Pray that we would think it important to encourage each other with Scripture.
- Pray that we would see part of being a Christian as being a provider, and not a consumer.
- Pray that we would not see service in the local church as being primarily about meeting our own felt needs by utilizing our giftedness but about bringing God glory.

- Pray that we would see it as unusual when the local church isn't the focal point of much of our energy and ambition.
- Pray that we would see it as unusual when a member's life seems to keep church on the periphery.
- Pray that we would see hospitality as an important part of being a Christian.

3. Work to Shape the Requests That Come from Your Congregation

Perhaps you have a weekly prayer meeting. Or perhaps your church is small and informal enough that members offer prayer requests during your main weekly gathering. In either case, these times of prayer can be wonderful. But they can also reinforce bad prayer habits. We should take care to shape these requests.

Consider allowing a pastor or elder to lead this time, with people letting him know ahead of time what they would like the church to pray for. That level of planning might dampen some of the intimacy of a prayer gathering. But this is where praying with the entire church is different from praying with your friends. After all, congregational prayer offers a whole different level of teaching and example. Just as we're careful who provides our congregation with sermon-based teaching, we should take care selecting who provides prayer-based teaching.

If you're the person who leads this prayer time, you may at times need to tell someone that a particular request isn't going to make the cut for congregational prayer. An aunt's friend's battle with cancer, for example. Praying for that is without doubt a good thing. Perhaps you pray for her right there on the spot, or encourage her to share the request with friends in the church. But you'll need to explain that with limited time together as a whole congregation, we can't pray for everything. Specifically, we want to prioritize those requests that are close to us as a congregation and those of the greatest eternal significance. These conversations may be awkward at times, but without them, you'll have a very difficult time shaping your congregation's priorities for prayer.

At other times, you'll need to recruit prayer requests. For example, I'm eager for our church to pray about fruit from good evangelistic work that we're doing. But for many it feels self-aggrandizing to tell the entire church about some good thing they've done. Of course, I would never tell people to share requests with the church if they didn't feel comfortable doing so. And for those tempted to share simply to impress others, a desire for humility may well be good reason to keep quiet. Yet oftentimes, wisdom argues for people to overcome their initial reluctance to share a request that might cast them in a positive light—for both their good and the congregation's.

How Should We Pray Corporately?

What we pray for matters. So does how we pray. It can strengthen or erode our unity. So how should we pray together?

Corporate Prayer Should Be Together

You'd be amazed at how often corporate prayer isn't actually corporate. Sometimes it feels less like a person is leading us in prayer—and more like we're just listening in. When corporate prayer is nothing more than listening in on someone else's quiet time, we don't actually pray. We become easily distracted, we don't labor with them in prayer, and we lose many of the benefits of corporate prayer. On the other hand, when someone *leads* the congregation in prayer, he or she serves us by structuring our prayer before God. A few simple practices can help a congregation recover the corporateness of corporate prayer.

- Pray *we* instead of *I*, just as Jesus did in the Lord's Prayer.
- Pray concisely. Jesus was clear: length in prayer is not necessarily a virtue. Often, in fact, brevity helps others pray with us rather than mentally checking out.

- Pray loudly. It seems like a small detail, but volume can help or hinder our prayer as a body.
- Say *amen*. When the whole congregation joins in the "amen" at the end of a prayer, we formally agree: "This was my prayer too!"

Corporate Prayer Should Be Exemplary

Corporate prayer serves as a model for how a congregation prays—both publicly and privately. Here are some thoughts on how to take full advantage of corporate prayer as a teaching opportunity:

For longer corporate prayers (like in your main weekly service):

- Make sure that those who lead these prayers can teach your people well. That doesn't mean that only elders can lead in prayer. But you want to think roughly in the same category as those you trust to preach to your congregation.
- Encourage leaders to think through their prayer ahead of time, perhaps jotting down a few notes. As much as evangelical church culture would suggest otherwise, there is nothing uniquely spiritual about extemporaneous prayer. The Spirit can lead through advance preparation just as well as in the moment.
- Encourage leaders to pray with a passion that fits their personality and the God they're addressing. Sometimes we plan our prayers so meticulously that they feel more read than prayed.
- Encourage a culture where it is normal to pray Scripture back to God. What better way can we ensure that our prayer honors God? And what better way can we shape the priority of our prayers according to God's own priorities? D. A. Carson's book, *A Call to Spiritual Reformation*, helps us model our prayers after those of the apostle Paul. It might be useful for someone learning to lead the congregation in prayer.

For shorter corporate prayers (like in a prayer meeting):

- Give a few minutes' notice before someone leads in prayer so he or she can pull some thoughts together.

- Select those who you trust will pray things that are true and honoring to God.
- Select those who will be able to lead the congregation into prayer. My congregation has a few very godly members who have difficulty speaking loudly and who cannot pray concisely. I deeply appreciate them. But I will probably not ask them to lead us in prayer as a congregation.

How Can We Pray for the Church in Private?

Despite the importance of corporate prayer, Jesus was clear that we should also pray in private (Matt. 6:6). The centrality of the local church to God's redemptive plan should lead your people to spend much of their prayer time interceding for your church. How can you encourage that? Well, if you've carefully structured times of corporate prayer, you're already building a compelling model. Beyond that, however, here are a few further ideas to help your church pray for your church:

- Encourage people to pray for those they know in the church. This comes quite naturally. Perhaps on **F**ridays you pray for your **f**riends within the church and non-Christian friends. Or **M**ondays you pray for the **m**en you know in the church and **W**ednesdays you pray for the **w**omen. In any case, part of loving a church is to pray for them.
- Encourage people to pray for those they *don't* know in the church. One of my church's most useful ministry tools is our pictorial membership directory. We encourage church members to pray through it once each month. To tell the truth, it feels strange at first when I pray for people I don't know well—or have never even met. But keep in mind that Paul prayed for the Roman Christians he'd never met simply because they were brothers and sisters in Christ (Rom. 1:8–10). It is a wonderfully God-honoring thing to invest time in prayer for those you have no emotional connection with—simply because they are part of your church family. And without knowledge of their specific circumstances, you may

actually end up praying larger, more important things for them. As a side benefit, if you're praying for people you don't know, you're more likely to recognize them when you do meet them. For churches that are trying to establish meaningful membership, a directory of members goes a long way to clarifying who is inside the church.

- Encourage people to pray for the preaching they hear. Even the apostle Paul asked for this: "[Pray] also for me, that words may be given to me in opening my mouth boldly to proclaim the mystery of the gospel, for which I am an ambassador in chains, that I may declare it boldly, as I ought to speak" (Eph. 6:19–20).

- Encourage people to pray for a biblical church culture. On the cover of our church directory, I've included the eleven elements of our church culture I referenced earlier in this chapter. These are good things for the entire congregation to ask God for on a regular basis—with the hope that we who pray would also demonstrate them.

Conclusion
Getting Practical

Preaching and prayer. These are God's ordinary means for accomplishing the supernatural in the local church. But precisely what kind of community does this environment foster? That's our next topic, as we consider first how to encourage our congregations to invest in relationships (chaps. 6 and 7) and then how to protect those relationships from disappointment and sin (chaps. 8 and 9).

7

Build a Culture of Spiritually Intentional Relationships

Could it be that the most active members of your congregation are the least fruitful? Consider for a moment: in God's sight, not all activity carries equal value. Not even all *church* activity. In 1 Corinthians 3, Paul uses the image of a farmer to describe the process of planting a church. "I planted, Apollos watered, but God gave the growth" (v. 6). Then as Paul transitions to the image of a builder to describe the growth of this church, it becomes clear that some church activity counts as worthless.

> According to the grace of God given to me, like a skilled master builder I laid a foundation, and someone else is building upon it. Let each one take care how he builds upon it. For no one can lay a foundation other than that which is laid, which is Jesus Christ. Now if anyone builds on the foundation with gold, silver, precious stones, wood, hay, straw—each one's work will become manifest, for the Day will disclose it, because it will be revealed by fire, and the fire will test what sort of work each one has done. If the work that anyone has built on the foundation survives, he will receive a

reward. If anyone's work is burned up, he will suffer loss, though he himself will be saved, but only as through fire. (3:10–15)

What a sobering picture. On the last day, God will reveal every action—even every word (Matt. 12:36)—for its true value. Despite the best of motives, some church activity will be judged as worthless.

In our churches, opportunities for wasted effort abound. Think of "fellowship" that is nothing more than virulent exchange of gossip. Think of people attending sermons and not listening. Think of endless rehearsals by a tone-deaf choir that, on further reckoning, merely distracts the congregation from worship. Think of cookbook sales, charity auctions, and 10 km races that consume enormous time for relatively small spiritual gain. All these things—fellowship events, sermons, choirs, and fund-raisers—*can* bear real spiritual fruit. But sometimes they don't.

In fact, church activity may especially attract the least spiritual. If there are any in your congregation who, like the Galatians, began "with the Spirit" but now seek to be "perfected by the flesh" (Gal. 3:3), they will likely be consumed with activity. What better shows that we are worthy of God's affection than throwing ourselves into activity at church? The infrastructure and inner workings of your church offer more than sufficient cover for the works-focused person to take shelter from the gospel. In fact, some of the most active members of your church may in fact be the least spiritual.

Value in Relationships

So where *can* we invest to bring about eternally lasting fruit? We can invest in spiritually intentional relationships. To revisit well-trodden ground in this book, love for other Christians shows us to be true Christians (1 John 2:10–11). Love for other Christians demonstrates the power of the gospel to the watching world (John 13:35). Love for other Christians makes for an eternally rewarding investment (Luke 16:9). Love for other Christians is primarily how we live out the fruit of the Spirit (Gal. 5:22–23).

As a general rule, church activity that builds into relationships will last; activity that doesn't, won't. After all, people are eternal; everything else will pass away. Of course, exceptions exist: we can erect infrastructure that supports the relational work of the local church (managing church financial records, for example). But by and large, the lasting work of the church is the relational work of the church.

But not any relationships will do. This chapter describes a culture of *spiritually intentional* relationships. The New Testament describes how Christians are to confront, to encourage, to discipline, to confess sin, and so forth. In the church, we want to see relationships where it is *normal* to talk about spiritual things. Not where conversation is never about football or kids or politics—but where a conversation with no spiritual grounding would be unusual.

How do we encourage this culture in our churches? This chapter will describe three strategies to foster a culture of spiritually intentional relationships. Chapter 8 will examine how we can remove structural impediments to such a culture shift.

Strategy 1
Advocate for Simple and Informal Relationships

Simply telling people to "invest in relationships" as a way to live out the Christian life is vague and impractical. "OK . . . so what exactly should I *do*?" Instead, it helps to paint a picture for the congregation of what spiritually intentional relationships look like. You might call these pictures "relational models." And the relational models that will best equip your people to catch this vision and run with it are those that are both simple and informal.

Keep It Simple

The New Testament authors repeatedly describe two different types of relationships between Christians. First, they describe mentoring relationships, which I'll refer to as discipling relationships.

These are relationships aimed at doing another person spiritual good. Paul's concern for Timothy and Jesus's care for his disciples are prime examples. Second, they address hospitality. Numerous passages encourage Christians to show each other hospitality—both to strengthen the local church (Rom. 12:13) and to support gospel workers (3 John 8). These two relational models are simple to grasp, simple to communicate, and simple to pass along. When you describe them to people, the idea of "being relational" becomes practical. Let me show you how each of these models helps reinforce a larger culture of spiritually intentional relationships.

Discipling. Encourage church members to meet together with other members on a regular basis to read a Christian book together, study a book of the Bible together, or simply encourage each other's spiritual life. The beauty of this focus is that the elements that make for a good discipling relationship (intentionality and a focus on each other's spiritual good) also make for a good church culture. Though discipling relationships may seem artificial at first, over time intentionality and spiritual focus become natural. And as those virtues blossom, they will spill over into all the other friendships a person has. To borrow language from the first chapter of this book, a church-wide habit of discipling builds *depth* of relationship into a church culture.

Hospitality. This is a second model of relationship in the New Testament. Once again, the habits Christians develop by exercising hospitality flow over into other relationships. Our culture defines hospitality very narrowly: "invite people over for dinner." But the New Testament use of the word is much broader. The original word, *xenophile,* literally means "lover of strangers."[1] So encourage people to think of hospitality more broadly. Inviting people out for a meal, walking up to a stranger at church to say hello, and attending the wedding of a church member you don't know—all these are

---

[1] I'm not suggesting that an English transliteration of the Greek word should govern our interpretation and application. But this broader interpretation of the word is consistent with how it's used in the New Testament.

hospitality. At my own church, one thing that accelerated a focus on hospitality was when college students began inviting families to their dorm rooms for ramen noodle dinners. You can't imagine a better opportunity for the gospel in a college dormitory than a family with little kids perched on the futon eating from Styrofoam. "How on earth do you know them?" When people grow in hospitality, they grow in inviting others into their lives. And they grow in reaching out to those with whom they don't share much natural affinity. This simple model of relationship helps shape a church culture. In this case, the result is a culture with relational *breadth*.

Keep It Informal

I remember a conversation with a pastor who'd caught a vision for discipling and wanted to see it happen in his church. So he put together a spreadsheet to pair every member of his church with someone else to meet up weekly. But I discouraged him from doing it this way. He might spawn some good discipling relationships, I told him. But he'd end up making discipling a church program rather than an element of his church's culture. Discipling should be a mind-set of spiritual intentionality that flows into all manner of friendships— not a program you "sign up for" and then do in a particular way. This pastor abandoned his spreadsheet, began advocating for a less programmatic approach, and has seen good fruit in his church as a result. The same holds true for hospitality. If you set up regular dinners as your way to program hospitality into the life of your church, you will undoubtedly see good fruit. But by squeezing a general biblical concept into a programmatic box, you forgo opportunity to see these habits spread across all of a person's relationships.

How to Advocate

If it's best to keep these relationships simple and informal rather than "programming" them, how can we encourage them? Here are a few ideas:

- *Plan these priorities into your personal time.* Suppose you started using several lunches each week to meet up with three or four individuals in your church to study the Bible or read a Christian book together. And you do the same with a few dinners each month at home. Beyond that, you encourage these people you're focusing time on to do the same with their own lunches and dinners. Before long, you'll discover a quiet insurgency of culture change that shifts how your church spends its time—with a high value on informal, relational ministry.

- *Encourage discipling and hospitality as how to get involved.* As a church leader, I'm sure you've had people ask how they can get more involved in your church. Or perhaps you're regularly addressing that question at a newcomers class. Instead of pointing first to volunteer opportunities or small groups, you might point to discipling and hospitality. Emphasize that this informal, relational ministry is far more critical to the mission of the church than most other ways in which people might spend their time.

- *Apply Scripture.* If you are the one preaching on a regular basis, your sermon is a great opportunity to advocate for discipling and hospitality. Let's say you run across the "one another" passages of the New Testament, or the idea that God creates a *people* through his Word in the Old Testament, or the vision of the heavenly assembly in Revelation. Hospitality and discipling can be primary application of any of these passages.

- *Choose leaders who live this way.* When you choose leaders—for the position of elder or some other position—consider their ministries of discipling and hospitality. Does a candidate have a track record of being used by God to positively influence the spiritual lives of others? Does he have a broad ministry through the congregation rather than a nearly exclusive focus on those most similar to him?

- *Recommend books about these priorities.* By God's grace, many books exist that describe informal ministries of discipling and hospitality. So buy them, read them with others in your congregation, and give them away frequently. Here are a few examples: *The Trellis and the Vine* by Colin Marshall and Tony Payne; *The Master Plan of Evangelism* by Robert E. Coleman; *One-to-One* by Sophie Peace; *The Disciple-Making Church* by Bill Hull; *One to One Bible Reading* by David Helm; and *Open Heart, Open Home* by Karen Mains. Good books are little time-release capsules of culture-transforming teaching that you can spread around your church. Give them away often (extracting in exchange a promise to read them), and bit by bit you will change how your people think about church.

Of course, discipling and hospitality can consume a great deal of time. Which brings us to our next tool for fostering a relationship-focused church culture.

Strategy 2
Advocate for Lives Centered on the Local Church

A quick skim through the New Testament leaves the unambiguous impression that the local church is exceedingly important in God's economy. It makes his gospel visible (John 13:35); it protects the vitality of our faith (Gal. 6:1–2); it safeguards us from self-deception (1 Cor. 5:4–5); and it grows us in love (Heb. 10:23–25). Consequently, a life centered on the community of the local church is significantly more likely to be lived strategically in God's sight than a life where the local church languishes as a peripheral detail.

Like a centrifuge, however, the faster life spins, the more church gets pushed to the outer edges of a Christian's life. Consider all the forces conspiring to minimize the importance of the local church:

- *Career.* The modern job market is nonstop, global, and incessantly competitive. Between trips out of town, late nights at work, and urgent deadlines, providing for a family can all but squeeze out space for relationships at church. In my business career before becoming a pastor I managed a team in six cities spread across three continents. No regular nine to five there! You might live in a city where stable careers with predictable hours are the norm. But for many, that way of life does not exist.

- *Location.* In an effort to find affordable housing, good education, and a manageable commute, church members may live across a wide metro area. The time and energy required to span that distance can seriously discourage relational investment.
- *Recreation.* Decisions to join a sports team, to buy a boat, and to spend summers away can all curtail investment in relationships at church.
- *Family.* For many families, it's their children's extracurricular commitments more than their own that regulate their capacity for church involvement. Beyond that, every Christian must weigh carefully their responsibilities to care for children, spouse, and extended family (Eph. 5:33; 6:4; Matt. 15:4–9) with the biblical priority of the "household of faith" (Gal. 6:10).

Yet a drift away from the local church is not inevitable! Lifestyles can change. You *can* influence your congregation's decisions over time. For most of your people, a wise life will be one *centered on the local church.* A typical Christian will make more of his life for the kingdom of God if he prioritizes his ability to invest in the local church when making career decisions, housing decisions, recreation decisions, and others. Here are four ways you can help:

1. *Sermon Application.* It's impossible to preach through the Scriptures without routinely highlighting the importance of the local church. If the church is so important to God, it ought to be important to us.
2. *Private Counsel.* Your advice on questions as diverse as, Should I move to a new city?, Which job should I take?, or, Should my son join the traveling soccer team? can all pivot around the same core principle: center your life on the local church. Is there a church in that new city where you know your family will thrive? How do you think those new work hours will affect your small group ministry? How often will he be out of town for Sunday games? You should not oppose everything that competes with the local church. But if you regularly raise this principle in conversations,

your congregation will more likely make godly and strategic life decisions.

3. *Examples.* Hold out as examples to the congregation those who structure their lives so they can build into the church. After all, many have forgone affirmation and advancement elsewhere in order to do this. Of particular importance is the example of those without visible and public ministries, but who invest well in relationships.

4. *Positive Instruction.* When people undervalue church involvement relative to things like career, location, and recreation, it's because they're pursing good things—just in the wrong way. So teach on those good things!

   - Teach on the biblical value of recreation and rest. Time away is not escape but refreshment—to enjoy God's good gifts and to recharge a believer to serve God better.
   - Teach on the value of locating yourself near your church—or if that's not possible, near other members of the church.
   - Teach on the dignity of work so that we can support our families and give to those in need—and on excellence in work as an opportunity to image our creative God.

   Your silence on the biblical value of work, home, recreation, and family will create a spiritual vacuum into which all manner of worldly values will rush. Should a member of your church take a job with extensive travel? Of course, the answer is "it depends." But don't let your people make these decisions without solid teaching on the eternal value of both sides of the tradeoff: the aspects of the intense job that yield eternal value on the one hand; the eternal value of relationships built at church on the other.

God *loves* his church! It is his glory made visible in this world and the centerpiece of his redemptive plan. Each Christian in your church will one day give account for a lifetime spent in Christ's service. You will serve your people well if you help them center their lives around the focal point of God's plan: the local church.

Of course, a life centered on the local church is a life of counter-cultural commitment. Where does that level of commitment come from? Let's move on to a third strategy for fostering a relationship-focused church culture.

Strategy 3
Emphasize the Privileges of Church Membership

As I noted previously, the pattern of this world is to commit only after we feel comfortable. But church membership tells us to commit to a body of believers simply because we're followers of Christ—even if we hardly even know them. In many ways, church membership parallels marriage. Increasingly, our world laughs at marriage because it encumbers "free" and "spontaneous" love. And so all the privileges of marriage—sex, living together, emotional intimacy, and so forth—get cherry-picked and enjoyed outside of covenant. But as Christians, we understand that true love thrives on commitment, and we can enjoy the privileges of marriage far better within the safe walls of covenant. Commitment and relationship are two sides of the same coin. Similarly, the covenant of church membership is the ecosystem in which a relationship-focused church culture can thrive.

It follows, then, that if you want to cultivate a culture of intentional relationships, you will need to make a big deal of membership. Rather than letting membership languish unnoticed in the background, make it front and center as the gateway to life in your church.

In a few paragraphs, I'll outline two ways to make membership meaningful: to restrict membership to regular attenders and to restrict church involvement to members. But first, let me address an argument against these practices: that they make church feel exclusive. Let's say that I convinced you with my arguments in chapter 3. That membership, as a formal recognition of all the commitments Christians make to others in a local church, is vital to the Christian life. That we don't simply make this commitment as we get comfortable in relationship; it functions as the entry point to relationship. Let's say I convinced you of all of that. But now as I describe strategies to *emphasize* membership—even to restrict many aspects of church involvement to members—you feel I've overplayed my hand. "Sure, membership is in the Bible. But if church is only about the Christians on the inside, how will it ever reach the non-Christians on the outside?" Why restrict small groups to members, for example, if that's a primary entry point into your church? Why insist on parking volunteers being members if volunteering is an easy way for newcomers to get involved? "If we want to reach our world for Christ, shouldn't our churches be outward-facing and inclusive rather than insular and exclusive?"

My response? This is a false dichotomy. There is no necessary conflict between reaching the lost with the gospel and drawing clear boundaries between those inside and outside the church. In fact, the surest path to evangelistic witness *is* exclusivity. Galatians 6:10 tells us to "do good to everyone, and *especially* to those who are of the household of faith."[2] "Especially" is the language of exclusivity. As this love within the family of faith burns brightly, it becomes a primary witness to the truth of the gospel (John 13:35; Eph. 3:10).

By way of analogy, if you want to heat a large room with a fireplace of burning coals, what do you do? Do you spread the coals evenly through the room? No! You push the coals together—and as they burn brighter and hotter, the fire's warmth fills the space. If you decide to follow the advice for fostering community that I've laid out in this book, you must believe that God's plan for reaching the lost is for local churches to burn brighter and hotter. You must believe that in the long run, the exclusivity that fuels a blazing hot community of believers can do far more gospel work than watering down breadth and depth of commitment in order to feel inclusive.

---

[2] If you have been convinced that the word translated "especially" is better translated "that is," that would further strengthen this argument.

- What is the most effective strategy for reaching the lost in your area? Is it to focus everything on seekers and turn Sunday mornings into an evangelistic outreach? No! Make your services accessible to unbelievers, but focus church on the maturing of believers. In time, the supernatural witness of their love for each other will be many times more provocative than seeker-focused services could ever be. Focus on more *and* better disciples—and recognize that better disciples are your best strategy for seeing more disciples.

- What is the most effective strategy for drawing uninvolved Christians into community? Is it to open the doors and welcome them into whatever activity they will attempt? No! Shut the doors to restrict involvement by those not ready to make the commitment of membership. Cultivate a community of committed believers that is far more attractive than any slate of activities you could offer.

- What is the most effective strategy for caring for weak sheep in your congregation? Is it to focus more pastoral time and attention on their needs and struggles? No! Care for weak sheep, to be sure—that will always be a part of every pastor's life. But know that a culture of committed, intentional relationships will lead the church to care far better for the weak and struggling in your flock than even the most dedicated pastor or leadership team.

As you emphasize meaningful membership, you may be accused of not caring about the lost. You may be accused of building a church that's only fit for "super Christians," of not caring for the weak. And for some, this critique is dead-on. In many churches, an insular focus on community belies a lack of concern for the lost. In many churches, a passion for the finer points of ecclesiology and biblical doctrine never translates into community that embraces the plight of the world outside. Just because you agree with what I've been writing doesn't mean that your desires are in the right place. Yet the fact that some apply this erroneously doesn't make a culture of meaningful membership any less biblical. In the long run, building up your church community to burn brighter and hotter will normally produce far more fruit than the flashier strategies suggested in its place.

Now with that as apologetic, let's consider two ways to make church membership meaningful.

1. *Restrict membership to regular attenders.* Membership hardly feels meaningful when dozens or even hundreds of "members" never show up. Now of course, some have good reasons for not attending church. The elderly, the sick, and those serving with the military or as missionaries are not the people I have in mind. Instead, I'm thinking of those on your membership rolls who long ago lost connection with your church. These people should no longer be members of your church, for your sake and theirs. My own church went through this process of cleaning up our membership roll some time ago: two older women in the congregation spent nearly a year trying to locate the four hundred members who no longer attended. Some had died; others were happily members of other churches and submitted letters of resignation. Some unfortunately had left the faith; many could not be found. And then in one educationally lengthy members meeting, we voted each of the remaining people out of membership as an act of discipline. It was an act of discipline because as best we knew, they had failed to obey Hebrews 10:25, which tells us not to forsake assembling together. Before this meeting we had taught extensively about the importance of membership—and the importance of making membership meaningful. So the congregation was ready. But the process was painful nonetheless.

You might think that only aging churches in the West have this problem of nonattending members. But that's not the case; nominal Christianity thrives in all manner of places. Recently, I spent a morning counseling the pastor and elders of a large house church in an Asian country where the government actively persecutes churches. One might think that of all the places in the world, an environment of persecution would be one place where no one would join a church unless they actually intended to follow Christ. But while this church had instituted membership just five years ago, 30 percent of the membership rarely if ever came to church. Why? Following Christ—and even joining a church—had once seemed attractive to these individuals. But over time, the pull of the world and the pressure of the State had conspired to reveal their faith as merely nominal. After all, for the most part, nominal Christians don't get persecuted. And so just like a hundred-year-old Baptist church in the American South, this church's membership was soon bloated by nonattenders.

To nurture a culture of intentional relationships, membership must become meaningful. And that starts by removing from membership those unwilling to fulfill their commitment as members.

2. *Restrict involvement to members.* Many churches have the opposite problem from bloated membership roles: attendance that dwarfs membership. A church becomes a comfortable place for newcomers to live "in community" without first making the basic commitment of membership. While that culture may feel warm and inviting, it gradually degrades the quality of community because it attempts community without commitment. This was my own church's experience in the years following our effort to remove nonattending members from our roles. What did we do? We began to restrict the benefits of community to members. So we told the congregation that only members could volunteer in the children's ministry. Only members could join a small group. Only members could serve as ushers. And so forth. We made some exceptions along the way. For example, we encourage brand-new Christians to get into small groups right away even while they're figuring out membership. But for long-time Christians, we require commitment to the entire body (which we see in Scripture) before committing to serve on a ministry team or join a small group (which is optional). We didn't put all these requirements in place at once, and they were preceded by hours of public teaching and private instruction. The best approach for you will no doubt differ from ours. But what matters is that as you emphasize

the privileges of membership, the delineation between those inside and outside the church will come into sharper focus (1 Cor. 5:12). As the importance of membership increases in a church, commitment grows, relationships flourish, and the church becomes that much more attractive to those looking in from the outside.

Conclusion
Four *P*'s to Put It All Together

As church leaders, it's tempting to seek structural solutions to cultural problems. We see something we'd like to change about the basic instincts and habits of our church, and we look for the policy we can write to fix it all. For example, consider my earlier example of instilling a culture of discipling by assigning each church member to a mentoring relationship. Or a church that tries to instill a culture of intentional relationships by requiring each member to join a small group. Or a church that tries to become more neighborhood-focused by "outlawing" small groups outside a fixed geographic area. *Sometimes* a structural change can be a helpful companion when shifting culture. But if church policy is your main tool for promoting a culture of intentional relationships, I fear that whatever changes you see will be short-lived. Instead, consider four *P*'s that can lead to persistent cultural change.

1. *Personal example.* Much of what I'm describing in this chapter is a culture change I saw happen in my own church. But this did not happen overnight; rather, it was a slow process trickling through the congregation. One person began investing intentionally in the lives of a few others, who in turn caught the vision and began living in the same way. A few people moved their homes nearer to the church— followed by more as the wisdom of that decision became evident. Do not undervalue the long-term power of good examples. Select church leaders who model the type of church culture you want (1 Pet. 5:3). Hold up as examples those faithful church members who invest in relationships even though they don't participate in many church

programs. And encourage your own friends in the church to be good examples themselves.

2. *Preaching.* Remember, the best church policies in the world cannot change the hearts of your congregation. Where does supernatural change begin? It begins with a spark of faith, ignited as our people hear the Word of Christ. Do not undervalue the ability of faithful preaching to change church culture.

3. *Prayer.* Ask God to do this supernatural work in your own church. Many times, prayer is the most practical thing you "do" to encourage change.

4. *Patience.* Watching a culture of intentional relationships take root can feel like watching paint dry. We must have faith in the ordinary means of grace. As we preach faithfully, pray, and model godly relationships, change will often happen. But as Christ's servants, our job is not to "effect change." It is to be faithful. We work diligently to guide our churches in the right direction. And then as much as we long for change, we can rest content with whatever pace our Lord deems best. In fact, the richest harvest from our toil may only become visible long after our time on earth is finished. As Charles Bridges said so well, "The seed may lie under the clods till we lie there, *and then spring up.*"[3]

Jesus taught that one mark of a true Christian is a desire to obey God's commands (John 14:15). Christians *want* to obey the "one another" commands in Scripture. In that sense, all I've written in this chapter merely helps Christians do what comes naturally to them—in their new nature. But what if we have structured our churches—from the design of staff positions to the objectives of our ministries—in ways that *inhibit* this natural growth of intentional relationships?

---

[3] Charles Bridges, *The Christian Ministry* (1830; repr., Edinburgh: The Banner of Truth Trust, 2006), 75. Emphasis added.

8

Structural Obstacles to Biblical Community

In 1981, the American Central Intelligence Agency uncovered an opportunity. Burrowed deep into the American defense industry, a Soviet agent had engineered a massive theft of technology. As the secretary of the Air Force later reflected, "in essence, the Pentagon had been in an arms race with itself."[1] But rather than simply shut down the operation, the CIA followed a different game plan: they become hackers. Soon, pieces of stolen American technology secretly contained an unexpected surprise—a digital Trojan Horse, so to speak.

The most spectacular casualty of this reverse-espionage was the Trans-Siberian pipeline. The new pipeline was so complex, it required control software beyond the Soviet Union's design capabilities. But that was hardly a problem for the Soviet KGB: why build it when you can steal it instead? With full knowledge of the Soviet plan, however, the CIA asked computer engineers to design the code to go haywire at some moment of its choosing. The CIA's intent? "We expected that the pipeline would spring leaks all the way from Siberia to Germany."[2] But what happened instead was on an entirely different scale.

---

[1] Steve Kettmann, "Soviets Burned by CIA Hackers?," *Wired News* (blog), March 26, 2004.
[2] Ibid.

In June of 1982, the computer code switched on and began running pumps at speeds far beyond the pipeline's design capabilities. Pressure in the pipe skyrocketed, pipe welds failed, and gas erupted into flame. To date, it is still the largest nonnuclear explosion ever caused by humankind. Amazingly, no one was killed. What does this have to do with church community? The Soviets wanted to change the economics of the oil industry—but they discovered that resistance to that change was designed into the inner workings of their pipeline. We want to see supernatural breadth and depth of community in our churches. But we often discover resistance that's designed deep into the fabric of our churches—from our philosophy of small groups, to staff job descriptions, to the composition of ministry programs. So think of this chapter as a top-to-bottom review of your church, an opportunity to identify and address structural resistance to biblical community. We'll start with church staff.

Church Staff

Structural Resistance: ministry positions designed to *do* ministry.
Corrective Action: redesign ministry positions to *facilitate* ministry instead.

The Danger of Church Staff

Have you ever thought about your church staff as "structural resistance" to biblical community? Consider the *negative* effect that staff might have on depth and breadth of commitment in the local church.

- *Depth:* With a competent staff in place, a congregation might pass over caring for each other in favor of letting "trained professionals" do the job. Over time, this shift dilutes the depth of commitment a congregation has for one other. So *without* staff, a grieving widow is cared for by the congregation in a way that strengthens the entire community. But when staff meet that need, the congregation limits its investment and loses an opportunity for unity.

- *Breadth:* A proliferation of staff positions enables ministry that's tailored to the needs of each segment of the congregation. Yet this comes at a cost: the resulting "ministry by similarity" hampers an appropriate expression of diversity in the church.

The fact that church staff pose a threat to biblical community doesn't mean we should fire them all. After all, passages like 1 Timothy 5:17 and Galatians 6:6 provide a biblical model for paid staff—especially for those whose main work is preaching and teaching. Instead, this potential hazard should inform how we construct staff positions.

Take as an illustration a friend of mine who has served as college pastor for two different churches. In the first church, his elders wanted to serve a burgeoning student population, so they hired my friend to *do* college ministry. He mentored college students, spent time on campus, and ran weekly student gatherings. But while this approach met a need of the students, it isolated them from the rest of the congregation. Over time, the students saw the church as little more than a place to hear sermons; their real growth came through the student ministry. Then, my friend took a job at a new church where his job was not to *do* college ministry but to *facilitate* it. Today he spends less time meeting with students and more time recruiting members of the congregation to invest in that work. He serves as a bridge between the church and the university: setting up relationships between students and church members on the one hand; speaking to students about the importance of the local church on the other. The result? Church members have started spending more time with students. Students join church small groups composed largely of nonstudents. Students are shifting career plans to stay in town after graduation so they can continue to invest in *their* church. In the first church, a staff position enabled good ministry to students but at the cost of community. In the second church, the staff position enabled good ministry by building breadth and depth of community.

The Purpose of Church Staff

Keep in mind the "golden chain" of Ephesians 4:11–16. Christ gives leaders to his church. Those leaders in turn "prepare God's people for works of service." As God's people do that ministry, the local church body is built up. And ultimately the congregation reaches unity and maturity. The goal of community (unity and maturity) comes as the *congregation* does ministry—equipped by their leaders.

But think of how frequently our goals for staff inadvertently subvert this vision. A pastor has an idea for a worthy ministry—perhaps a mentoring program at a local school—and hires staff to help it grow. At first, things work well. The ministry blossoms, people in the church volunteer, and dozens of local youth hear the gospel. But eventually, interest begins to wane, and so ministry staff double up efforts to recruit volunteers. Staff become frustrated with church leadership for not promoting the ministry more forcefully. A band of loyal volunteers feels overtaxed trying to keep things running and struggles with resentment against those in the congregation who aren't involved. The more staff time the pastor throws at the mentoring program, the more he teaches the congregation that ministry is his responsibility and not theirs—discouraging their involvement even more. Instead of preparing God's people for works of service, staff get in the way.

Stop Outsourcing Ministry to Your Staff

In my experience, the most common way that church staff undermine community is when they usurp the church's opportunity to build unity through service—as in the examples above. So think through your staff individual by individual and jot down a rough approximation of time spent *doing* ministry (caring for weak sheep, mentoring new believers, sharing the gospel, etc.) versus *facilitating* ministry (training church members to better engage in ministry, coordinating pastoral care, preaching,[3] etc.). Under no circumstances

---

[3] Note that I list Word ministry (like preaching) as *facilitating* ministry and not *doing* ministry. That's because teaching God's Word is the primary way that leaders "equip the saints for the work of minis-

should church leaders entirely shift away from *doing* ministry. But like the apostles in Acts 6:2, we must understand the pressure for us to "give up preaching the word of God to serve tables." Consider a few approaches to avoiding this pitfall:

- *Remind staff that their job is to facilitate ministry and not to do ministry.* When we hired a PhD biblical counselor several years ago, this is what we told him. If after five years he was carrying the same counseling load as in year one, he was not doing his job. Instead, we wanted him to invest much of his time in training lay counselors. Both counseling and training are important. Yet given our neediness as a church, near-term crises will always crowd out longer-term training unless we deliberately push the other way. Staff should use their time and skills to "cut up" ministry into bite-sized chunks for your congregation to pursue.
- *Resist hiring staff to relieve congregational guilt.* In some areas of ministry, congregations chronically abdicate their responsibility—and feel guilty as a result. Typical examples include evangelism, care for the poor, and youth ministry. In these important but neglected areas of ministry, congregations love to put money toward staff—if only so they can feel that something is "getting done." But the wise church leader will resist hiring staff in these situations, choosing instead to teach, model by example, and pray for the Spirit to convict and conform the congregation. Then, once a pattern of ministry imprints into the congregation's DNA, they may hire staff to facilitate that ministry. "But wait!" you say. "Can't it be useful to hire staff to kick-start ministry among the congregation?" Hypothetically, yes. But I've actually seen relatively few situations where this works as intended. In general, it's best to take the longer road of waiting until you see initiative among the congregation before creating a staff position. It's just too easy for a busy congregation to relax their initiative once they hire someone to oversee an important priority.

---

try" in Ephesians 4:11–16. After all, the one commonality that "apostles, prophets, evangelists, shepherds, and teachers" all share is that they are ministers of God's Word.

- *Encourage the congregation to initiate ministry.* I love the repeated refrain in the book of Titus to teach the people to "be ready to do whatever is good" (3:1, cf. 1:8, 2:3, 14; 3:8, 14). Paul told these Christians in Crete to seize opportunities for good whenever they came along: to be flexible and entrepreneurial. If as a church leader you have a good idea for a new ministry, hand it off to someone else rather than announcing it in bright lights from the front. The up-front approach may get things started quickly, but it will teach your congregation to rely on their staff to figure out how to live out God's Word. A more organic approach may have a slower start, but it will invest your congregation with the joy and responsibility of ministry.

The Church Calendar

Structural Resistance: a weekly schedule of activity that crowds out informal relationships.

Corrective Action: consider the relative value of unprogrammed time when adding activities to the calendar.

The False Promise of a Crowded Schedule

Participation in church activities can be more comfortable than the hard work of building relationships. And an overfilled weekly calendar of events only exacerbates the problem. Sunday I'm at church. Monday night I meet with my small group. Tuesday is choir rehearsal. Wednesday I help with kids' club. Thursday I'm at our weekly theology class. Friday night I take my wife out on a date, and Saturday evening (after an exhausting schedule of soccer and Little League games) I watch the kids so she can prepare her Sunday school lesson. And now you want me to find time to build relationships with my non-Christian coworkers, meet up regularly with a brother to disciple him, form a friendship with a more mature Christian man, and invest in relationships with people in my church to the level that they are at times painful and inconvenient? Life is crazy enough, thank you very much!

You get the picture. Economists talk about the concept of "opportunity cost." In a world with fixed resources, saying "yes" to something always means saying "no" to something else. Everything has opportunity cost: the value of what you would otherwise have done. No activity on your church calendar is safely neutral. And when an activity's opportunity cost is the chance to form spiritually deliberate relationships, it's rarely worth the trade-off.

But making time for relationships is much more than simply canceling a few events on the official church calendar. We need a culture change, not just a scheduling change. Let me share an example to show why.

Recently a friend came to our church staff with an idea. She wanted to gather together recipes from all the women in the church, collect them into a cookbook that she could sell to church members, and give the proceeds to our local crisis pregnancy center. A good thing? Of course. But what is the opportunity cost? Why not encourage people to give money to the pregnancy center on their own? Why not spend the hundreds of hours of "cookbook time" having non-Christian friends over for dinner and discipling believers in the church? Would a cookbook be a fun thing to do? Certainly (at least for some people). Would it raise marginally more money for the pregnancy center? Probably. But at what cost?

And so I worked gently to dissuade her from this idea.

Think of the hundreds of good ideas like this that percolate up from your congregation, and you begin to comprehend the scale of the challenge. I mentioned in the last section that we want ministry to be entrepreneurial. Well, this is one challenge of a godly, entrepreneurial church. Your job is to teach your people the judgment to say "yes" to the right things and "no" to the next-best things.

How can you do this? Here are a few ideas:

- Track all the activities you're promoting as a church. It's a simple yet revealing exercise. You've got a problem if you can't see how a hypothetical, mature believer can navigate through the maze of "expected" activities while still leaving time for relationships. Perhaps that "hypothetical, mature believer" with a calendar stocked full of church events is you!

- Give your pastor control over which activities get promoted and how. This could include control over the list of announcements at your Sunday service, your church e-newsletter, communication passed through small group leaders, or your church website. Then over time see if he can't raise the bar for what gets on that list.

- Reconstitute existing ministries to be more relational in nature. Let's say you've got a potluck dinner that isn't much more than a monthly gab-fest advertised as "fellowship." Meanwhile, your church is within walking distance of an apartment complex with several hundred international students. Why not suggest to potluck leaders that they recast their event as an outreach to students? Students come for a free meal to practice their English; table leaders guide conversation in an evangelistic direction. Suddenly, there's another event on the church calendar you're excited about.

- Make it clear to your congregation that it's OK for things to die. No ministry is so valuable that it must continue in perpetuity. For example, if someone wants to do a weekly Bible study at a local prison, you'll gladly get behind it. But if the congregation eventually shifts their involvement to other things, don't put the prison ministry on life support and harass people until you get volunteers. Just let it die. An entire congregation of Spirit-filled believers now sees more God-glorifying ways to invest their time. That just might indicate that the ministry landscape has shifted. We want to see initiatives arise organically and then fall away when it's time to move on—except where we think the congregation is missing something.

- Look for strategic opportunities to kill unfruitful activities. If your congregation is more than a few years old, you're bound to find some activities that don't seem to bear much spiritual fruit. My advice? Be patient, but be active. A resource constraint here and a key volunteer disappearance there, and you'll guide people to activity that's more fruitful without spending much of their trust.

- Weigh opportunity cost when considering a new initiative. Keep in mind that most of the truly valuable ministry in your congregation is informal. It is members meeting together over coffee, having each other over for dinner, praying with each other on the phone, and so forth. Some new initiatives proposed by your members will serve to prosper and extend that informal ministry. Other ideas will get in the way. Gently guide members toward the first and away from the second.

- Look for what's better, not just what's best. Perhaps you're saying, "I agree with you. I'd love for my congregation to be consumed with vital, relational ministry. But right now, I'd just settle for them doing anything at all. Our monthly potluck may not be producing much spiritual fruit, but at least it's something!" I get it. And to you, I'd encourage you that God has sent you to shepherd the congregation you have, not to aim for an unrealistic ideal. Look for what spiritual good you *do* see in what they do, and encourage it. Then look for small ways to adjust those activities over time to see more of the good and less of the not-as-good. Steady, incremental change often accomplishes dramatically more than any of us predict at the outset. Remember: even when the farmer is asleep, the seed of the Word continues to grow (Mark 4:26–29). God is *always* at work.

By supporting some ideas, letting others alone, and quietly encouraging some to fade away, you can help your congregation escape the tyranny of a crowded church calendar. And you lead them to invest their time in a way they will be glad to give account for on the last day.

Church Music

Structural Resistance: music that's better performed than congregationally sung.

Corrective Action: aspire to a musical style that a broad range of people can use.

Your musical style says much about the type of church community you want to see. Let's say you design your music to attract people to your church. In doing so, you may simply teach people to come as consumers and not as providers. If you aim your music at a tight demographic scope (e.g., "We design our music for the twenty-something artistic crowd"), you will teach your people that homogeneity is desirable. If your music only ever speaks about happiness, joy, and victory in the Christian life, you suggest that those feeling differently aren't particularly welcome. And if your music never breaks out of any one era of Christian history (the 1990s praise song era; the 1600s Puritan hymn era), you teach your people that your church is only for people who like that kind of music.

Three errors of musical style can stifle community:

1. Music that's difficult to sing corporately. If your music appeals strongly to the taste of American twenty-somethings, you'll get a lot of accolades from American twenty-somethings. But the African Christian in her fifties may feel decidedly out of place. If you want music that embraces the natural diversity the gospel brings to a congregation, you'll need to think hard about your goals for musical style. Consider the cultural backgrounds of your congregation. Consider the cultural backgrounds of the non-Christian neighbors you hope to see in your church. How difficult is it for this diversity of people to sing the songs you choose? One factor at play is rhythmic complexity. Many Christian songs you hear on the radio are rather complex from a rhythmic standpoint. That's part of what makes them interesting. But that syncopation and changing meter and tempo may make them difficult for some in your congregation to learn—and especially those who come from cultural backgrounds where rhythmic simplicity is the norm. Unless your congregation is in a setting where musical complexity is common, you'll generally find that rhythmic simplicity will make your music accessible to the

widest variety of people. When you shape your musical style with the entire congregation in mind, you battle a consumerist mind-set that wants music that "appeals to me." And you emphasize the breadth of community we should expect to find in a local church.

2. Music with limited emotional breadth. Much of church music is happy music. But if that is all we ever have, we substantially dilute the Christian experience. And the tone we set in our services will inevitably carry over into relationships. If we teach people through our music that feelings of doubt, despair, and bewilderment are not acceptable starting points for worship, we teach them that these topics are not acceptable in private conversation either—to the detriment of depth in relationships. I tell new members at our church that I want music that helps them worship God if they got engaged the previous evening, and I want music that helps them worship God if they broke up the previous evening. When you select music with a variety of emotional starting points, you teach your congregation that God's promises hold true no matter our emotional condition.

3. Music that feels like a performance. Revelation 5:13 pictures the worship of heaven as the song of an entire congregation. Our churches should provide a foretaste of that. Musical accompaniment can help by leading us in song and helping us through sections of songs that are more difficult to sing. Or it can overpower congregational worship and turn us from active worshipers into passive listeners. Consider the volume and complexity of your musical accompaniment: does it help congregational worship? Or do people mumble softly while listening to the worship band or the organ? To be sung well, some melodies require an exceptionally talented congregation and accompaniment. Yet good congregational melodies can work without accompaniment. If you don't already, try going *a cappella* (without accompaniment) on the last verse or chorus of some of your songs. Little can build a feeling of congregational unity more than hearing the whole church sing their hearts out in passionate praise to God. We should design our musical style with this in mind.

Above all, we must teach our congregations that congregational worship requires sacrifice. That's why the corrective action at the beginning of this section is *not* "aspire to a simple musical style that a broad range of people *love*" but that a broad range of people *can use*. If we're serious about displaying the diversity that the gospel brings to a local congregation, then each of us will make sacrifices in the type of music we sing. Some may need to work to enjoy a particularly simple style of music. Some may need to work harder to worship God on Sunday morning. But through that small sacrifice, we enable congregational unity that sings a much more profound note of praise than any individual could ever produce on his own. And having experienced that taste of heaven, your congregation will gladly make the sacrifice.

Church Services

Structural Resistance: service schedules packed so tightly that people are rushed in and out.
Corrective Action: create space in the schedule for the congregation to congregate.

Time Following the Service

How you run your schedule on Sundays says much about what you expect of your people. What if they're ushered from the parking lot to the nursery and right into your theater-like seating area—then gently rushed out afterward to make space for the next service? It says that church is primarily about the experience of what happens during the service rather than the relationships that form around the service. So think through what your schedule says about your expectations. You can do simple things like place refreshments around the building after the service finishes to encourage people to stay around afterward to talk. Some churches provide the opportunity to share a meal after the service. Leave breathing room in the schedule before and after the service so people have time to talk. Then speak of the importance of coming early to the service and staying around afterward. Consumers rush in and out of the service, viewing church as a spiritual "drive-thru." But providers show up early and, as able, stay around afterward. They see church more as family and less as an event.

Second Weekly Gathering

Some churches have two services each week—the main gathering on Sunday morning, for example, and another meeting on Sunday night or Wednesday night. For those with the option, a second weekly gathering offers rich opportunity to foster community. Instead of making it a virtual duplicate of your Sunday morning service, consider turning it into "church family" time. Provide time for individual church members to share prayer requests and to ask for help. Provide time to lift these needs up in prayer.

Even though this isn't "fellowship time" in the typical sense of the word (informal time spent talking together), it fosters fellowship in the church. A second weekly gathering can help foster community in three important ways.

1. It allows people to know what is spiritually significant in the life of the entire church. Though you can't know what's going on in everyone's life, you know the headlines, so to speak. That increases a sense of belonging and commitment—commitment not just to the few people you know well but to the entire church that God has assembled together.

2. It helps people learn about each other, which helps them form connections outside of church services. You hear of a ministry you could get involved in, or a need you could meet, or an experience that strikes a chord with your own. These are opportunities for deeper connections with people you might otherwise never have met.

3. It allows people to share the experience of praying earnestly for God to work, week after week, and then seeing him answer.

You'll likely face some reluctance if you're resurrecting a moribund second weekly gathering or trying to create one from scratch. But be patient and sell people on the vision of what you're trying to do. You want to create a church that feels like a family.

Demographic-Based Ministries

Structural Resistance: demographic-based ministries that substitute for church-wide community.

Corrective Action: manage these ministries to emphasize the upside and limit the downside; reprogram them to serve the entire church.

One main way modern churches build community is by dividing the congregation along demographic lines. A singles ministry aims for one segment of the congregation; small groups for young moms serve another; a weekly dinner for retired couples builds community for a third; morning gatherings for artists help yet another, and so on. These are what I refer to as "demographic-based ministries." As I've pointed out elsewhere in the book, these kinds of groupings can be beneficial to the life of a church. It's helpful to be around Christians who understand me because they're similar to me. The problem is when community consists of little more than demographic segmentation; that kind of community fails to display the power of the gospel.

Specifically, two challenges confront nearly every demographic-based ministry.

- Challenge 1: they can hinder depth of community. People love ministry programs custom-built for people "just like them." And therein lies the problem. Every church battles a consumerist mindset. When a church forms community based on demographic groupings, it essentially says that church is "all about me." If I'm a young single, I'm ushered into the young singles group where ministry is geared toward the needs of young singles. In managing demographic-based ministry, we must be careful not to encourage a consumerist mindset.

- Challenge 2: they can hinder breadth of community. The reason why demographic-based ministry "works" so well is that people are more comfortable with others who are just like them. But, as we saw earlier in this book, this kind of community proclaims significantly less about the gospel than community among people who have nothing in common but Jesus. Church community will include relationships of similarity—but should never be characterized by them.

Here are two suggestions for your demographic-based ministries.

1. *Consider the cost/benefit of these ministries and manage accordingly.* For years, my wife and I have led a small group limited to newly married couples. That's the one exception my church has made to the rule that small groups not be defined by life stage. Why? Because the first years of marriage are so critical, we've decided that the benefits are worth the costs for newly married groups. That is, the benefit of specific teaching and mentoring during these years is worth the cost of segmenting the congregation along demographic lines. But having recognized this cost, we work hard to manage it. We limit the groups to two years. No matter how well a group has "gelled," when the two years are up, we disband the group. And given the cost we're incurring to church unity, we've tried to accentuate the benefits of these groups by increasing investment in group leaders and curriculum. The last thing we want is a demographically limited small group that isn't accomplishing very much.

Of course, this cost/benefit assessment will be different depending on your church. If you're in a church that has a particular struggle with all the young married couples hanging out exclusively with each other, you might decide that despite all its benefits, this type of small group isn't actually worth the cost. Or if you're in a church with a "church exists for me" mind-set, you may find that selectively removing some of these demographic boundaries can help turn your people from consumers to providers. So look across your singles group, your college-aged Sunday school class, your moms-of-preschoolers group and ask three questions:

1. What benefit are you getting from this demographic grouping of the congregation? Your standard should be higher than "more people come because they enjoy being with people just like them."
2. Based on the state of your church culture, is this benefit worth the cost to breadth and depth of community?
3. How can you structure these ministries to accentuate the benefits and minimize the costs?

2. Reprogram existing ministries to serve the entire church. For many years, our church has taught a class on parenting. A few years ago, the teacher came to me and suggested that the class be retitled "Parenthood" instead of "Parenting." At first I thought this was odd. After all, who actually uses that word? But as he explained the changes he was making to the class, I was delighted. "Parenting" is a class geared toward parents on how to parent. Nothing wrong with that. But a class called "Parenthood" does better by teaching on a topic every Christian should understand—be they parents or not. After all, God refers to himself as our Father. Doesn't learning about parenthood help us understand that more fully? And while the majority of our congregation may not be parents, they are called to love and care for the minority who are. A shift from "Parenting" to "Parenthood" transformed this class from a narrow demographic focus to something that can serve the entire church. And sure enough, over the years the portion of nonparents attending this class has swelled.

Is there some reprogramming that would benefit your own church culture? Could you make your singles group less about creating community for singles and more about integrating families into the lives of single adults? Or let your pastor for families spend as much time teaching single adults about healthy families as he does coordinating children's ministry? Remember that as you do this, you not only address the breadth of community in your church, but its depth as well. You're teaching people that church isn't fundamentally about meeting their needs, but about how they can serve those with whom they may not share much in common other than Christ.

Conclusion

Don't Lean on Any One Ministry to Cultivate Community

One reason we end up with all these structural obstacles to community in our churches is that we have too narrow an understanding of what it takes to grow community. I've talked with pastors who see small groups as *the tool* for building community in their churches. Or who see demographic-based ministries as *the way* they will foster community. In other words, if we don't have strong community, we start a ministry to check that box. "Insert small groups. Now we have community!"

But when we do this, we're in essence relying on a new ministry to reprogram an entire church culture. Surely that will never work! Reinventing small groups won't address structural obstacles to community that exist elsewhere in our churches. Launching new demographic-based ministries won't change how our people think about their relationships, or what it means to be a church, or what it means to be a Christian. If, however, we view the task of fostering community as an exercise in shaping church culture, we will take advantage of every opportunity to encourage people toward spiritually significant relationships—from the preaching ministry to staff job descriptions to the church calendar to our philosophy of small groups. If the battle for community is a battle for church culture, we must wage it on all fronts.

Speaking of battle, you may have noticed that these last two chapters have described community without much reference to our main enemies in the Christian life: the world, the flesh, and the Devil. As hard as it is to cultivate community, it is critical that we recognize the enemies at work trying to tear it down. How we protect community is the topic of our next two chapters.

Part 3

Protecting Community

9

Addressing Discontentment in the Church

Istanbul's Hagia Sophia stands as one of antiquity's most intriguing structures. It was remarkable in AD 532 when Emperor Justinian opened it as the world's largest cathedral—a title it would hold for a thousand years. But the Hagia Sophia is even more remarkable for what it has done in the years since, because it is a *self-healing* church. Originally fashioned from extraordinarily hearty cement from an island in the Mediterranean, the mortar in its walls has never fully set, even a millennium and a half later. When earthquakes strike (as they often do in Istanbul), and cracks and fissures open up in the structure, they remain only until the next downpour. Then water seeping through these cracks sets the ancient cement, sealing the mortar tight. It's a far more effective repair regimen than any engineer could devise.[1]

And it provokes the imagination. A "self-healing church." What if cracks and fissures in your congregation closed up all by themselves? What if the basic culture of your church leaned strongly toward

[1] Virginia Hughes, "Shaken, Not Stirred," *Nature* 443 (September 2006): 390–91, doi:10.1038/443390a.

unity? So far in this book, we've discussed how to foster community in the local church with supernatural breadth and depth of commitment—community that proclaims the glory of God. Now we turn to protecting that community. How can a congregation address the myriad obstacles to unity that inevitably arise so that, like the Hagia Sophia, it becomes a self-healing church?

God's Strange Design

This chapter and the next address a spiritual conundrum that awaits us in the Scriptures—a conundrum that boils down to three simple biblical facts.

- Fact 1: God has called Christians to be with him forever. But for a time, he's left us in this world, gathered into local churches (Heb. 10:25).
- Fact 2: God intends our life together to show off his wisdom and power (Eph. 3:10).
- Fact 3: We are sinners (Rom. 5:12).

The first two facts work quite well together; the third complicates matters considerably. Yet in God's inscrutable wisdom, he has left the task of displaying the glory of his *perfect* character to the very *imperfect* people of his church.

So how can we live out God's plans for us despite our sin? Chapter 10 will discuss sin against each other in the church. The chapter you're reading now will examine a different fruit of the fall: discontent. So often, threats to church unity don't come from offenses against one another, but disappointed expectations and perceived rejection. As Proverbs 13:12 says, "Hope deferred makes the heart sick." By addressing sin in one chapter and discontent in another, I'm not denying that discontent often comes from sin or becomes sin. After all, the root of discontent is often the idolatry that lies deep in every human heart. But a wise response to discontentment will differ from one that is about a specific offense. Thus a chapter on each.

Discontent is inevitable; broken unity is not. So how do we help our churches address discontent? The first half of this chapter will examine Acts 6 as a study in how church leaders can shepherd a congregation through a threat to church unity. Then, in the second half, we'll consider how we can prepare our churches for these difficult times.

Leading through Times of Discontent

In the book of Acts, just four chapters after Pentecost, discontent threatens the unity of the first church. The way the apostles lead is instructive:

> Now in these days when the disciples were increasing in number, a complaint by the Hellenists arose against the Hebrews because their widows were being neglected in the daily distribution. And the twelve summoned the full number of the disciples and said, "It is not right that we should give up preaching the word of God to serve tables. Therefore, brothers, pick out from among you seven men of good repute, full of the Spirit and of wisdom, whom we will appoint to this duty. But we will devote ourselves to prayer and to the ministry of the word." And what they said pleased the whole gathering, and they chose Stephen, a man full of faith and of the Holy Spirit, and Philip, and Prochorus, and Nicanor, and Timon, and Parmenas, and Nicolaus, a proselyte of Antioch. These they set before the apostles, and they prayed and laid their hands on them.
>
> And the word of God continued to increase, and the number of the disciples multiplied greatly in Jerusalem, and a great many of the priests became obedient to the faith. (Acts 6:1–7)

In Ephesians 3, Paul argues that unity between Jew and Gentile is a glorious demonstration of the power of the gospel. The composition of the Jerusalem church in Acts 6 isn't quite that; the "Hellenists" and "Hebrews" (as the ESV translates the terms) were likely both Jews. The Hellenists were Jews from across the Roman Empire who had gathered in Jerusalem for Pentecost; the Hebrews were Jews from Palestine. Hellenists would have been more comfortable in Greek culture, Hebrews in Jewish culture. Hellenists would have been more comfortable speaking in Greek, Hebrews in Aramaic.[2] Contemporary historians wrote about the animosity between the two.[3] So unity between the two would have been remarkable.

The gospel asserts that unity in Christ is stronger than worldly difference. The apostles faced a natural fault line that threatened that assertion. And their response suggests several principles that can help us address discontent in our own contexts.[4]

1. *Threats to church unity deserve the attention of church leaders.* Many in the first century would have dismissed unequal treatment of widows as insignificant. But the issue was significant enough to the apostles that they gathered "the full number of the disciples" to discuss it—which may well have numbered in the thousands. Why was this problem so important? Luke's emphasis in these verses seems to be on the "complaint" of verse 1. The complaint wasn't merely about inequity; it was an inequity that threatened church unity. Just think: nearly every Christian on earth was called into that meeting. That's how important widows are; that's how important unity is. Unity is precious, but unity is also precarious. When unity is threatened, church leaders should take notice.

2. *But ultimately, it is the congregation's job to protect unity.* You might think that because of how important this issue was, the apostles would take charge of things themselves. But they don't. "It is

---

[2] I. Howard Marshall, *The Acts of the Apostles* (1980; repr., Grand Rapids, MI: Inter-Varsity Press; Eerdmans, 2000), 125–26.

[3] K. C. Hanson and Douglas E. Oakman, *Palestine in the Time of Jesus: Social Structures and Social Conflicts* (Minneapolis: Augsburg Fortress, 1998), 149.

[4] For the next few pages, I make some principled application to churches today based on what the apostles did in Acts 6. In doing this, I'm not suggesting that every apostolic action in Acts is a binding pattern for the local church today. For example, I believe that all churches should have deacons. But I don't believe that simply because we see deacons in Acts 6. Rather, I believe that because the Epistles assume that this office will exist in local churches. First Timothy 3 lays out qualifications for the office, and Philippians 1:1 references deacons as a particular group of leaders in a church. But while the *office* of deacon seems to be a normative pattern for us to follow, *how* the apostles inaugurated this office is not repeated elsewhere in Scripture. I'm not suggesting that the six observations I'm about to make are required of today's churches. I'm simply trying to apply wisdom that I see in the apostles' decisions to similar challenges we might face in our own churches.

not right that we should give up preaching the word of God to serve tables." All the apostles do is to address the congregation. The solution will come from seven men, not from the apostles. Seven men whom the church is to select, not the apostles. Essentially, the apostles tell the congregation: "This issue is too important to ignore. But it is not important enough to distract us from the ministry of the Word. Go solve it yourselves!"

Leaders must lead, but protecting unity is ultimately the church's responsibility. After all, who does Paul urge in Ephesians 4:3 to be "eager to maintain the unity of the Spirit in the bond of peace?" The congregation. Too often, Christians throw problems straight to church leaders for resolution. As a leader, you won't serve your church well if you assist them in abdicating their responsibility. Instead, you should lead the congregation to address its own unity problems.

Recently, a new church member came to me because he'd felt left out during his first few months at the church. But, much to my delight, he also came with some ideas of how to help future members integrate better into our church community. And what's more, he felt he had the time to put some of his ideas into practice. What a wonderful example of helping leaders to lead, while at the same time owning his part in building unity.

3. Be reluctant to take sides. In Acts 6, the apostles seem careful to avoid aligning themselves with either the Hellenist or Hebrew side of the controversy. It doesn't appear that the apostles even attempted to determine if the Hellenist widows *were* being neglected; the mere perception of favoritism required action. There was no caucusing of the congregation, with the apostles meeting first with the Hellenists and then with the Hebrews. Instead, Luke records that "the twelve summoned the *full number* of the disciples." Then, when they speak to the congregation, they make no mention whatsoever of the division that fed the conflict. And the apostles' advice, that *seven* men be chosen, precludes the kind of compromise that would lead to equal participation by Hellenists and Hebrews. Instead, the apostles challenge the congregation to address this problem as a single body. The apostles are not blind to the division that created the conflict. But their choice of action ensures that in no way will division be enshrined in the resulting solution.

This principle is useful in our own contexts. So often, we have limited visibility into the root of complaints that people bring us. For example, someone complains that the church "doesn't care about the poor." If that were true, God help us! But I cannot even know my own heart and motives, let alone those of an entire congregation. Yet I don't need to judge the truth of that accusation in order to lead toward unity. Instead, I should take widespread perception of favoritism as a problem, irrespective of whether someone is actually at fault. Then I should lead the congregation in considering how they can better care for each other, without reference to the specific factions of rich and poor.

4. *Act in response to tangible, structural problems.* A friend of mine put it this way: "It's noteworthy that beyond teaching that stressed the unity of all Christians in Christ, it was not until a structural issue arose that the Apostles took any recorded action. One could . . . read this to mean that the Apostles didn't really care about the issue. Or, it could be that they understood that structural solutions only work to deal with specific structural problems."[5] As church leaders, we often hear from unhappy people. Too often, we feel our job is to make everyone happy. But that is neither realistic nor biblical.

In contrast to our desire to please everyone, the apostles' example is enlightening. Given all the mistrust and tension between the Hellenists and Hebrews that we know of from the first century, it seems unlikely that this was the first time the two groups had run into difficulty. But it appears that, rather than responding to a general sense of discontent or discomfort, the apostles were slow to act until they saw an issue that was structural and tangible.

---

[5] Andrew Johnson, unpublished memo on ethnocultural relations in the local church.

The same guideline can help us respond to discontent in our own churches. As a pastor, when someone approaches me about feeling left out, misunderstood, or undervalued, I have a great desire to "fix things." But often the action that I would take would merely make things difficult elsewhere in the congregation—or even for that person. And I never want to be in a situation where I "lead" by merely responding to those who complain the loudest. Generally, we are wise to listen patiently to those experiencing challenges with our churches. But we should wait to apply any kind of solution until we see a tangible fix to a tangible problem.

Here's an example from my own experience. As my church grew up from a church of mainly young singles to a church with more families, some families complained that the church ignored their unique needs and schedules. As you can imagine, some of that concern was expressed in a godly and loving manner; other times it was less mature. Our elders talked through this demographic change we were experiencing. But we didn't find much that we should change other than reminding both singles and families that part of living together in a local church is sacrificing our interests for the benefit of others.

Then one family pointed out that moving our service forward by an hour would make it much easier for families with school-aged kids. The elders surveyed a cross section of the congregation to see how that change would affect people in different life stages and geographies. Sure enough, the change would make life easier for young families without much negative impact on the rest of the congregation. So we made the change.

I have often been thankful when my elders have been willing to listen to discontented people—and consider what might be done—but wait to act until they see a tangible solution to a tangible problem.

5. *Temper expectations for what church leaders can do.* One word that strikes me as I read these verses in Acts 6 is the word *neglected*. It appears that the goal of the apostles' action was not equality or comfort

for all but the end of favoritism: the avoidance of one group being neglected. Frankly, at first glance, that ambition is underwhelming. I'm sure the apostles would have loved to see more people do what Barnabas did in Acts 4:37 when he sold an entire field and laid the money at their feet. That's the kind of thing that gets you excited! But instead of aiming high like that, the apostles merely seek to avoid neglect.

In this, we see the wisdom of setting appropriate expectations for what church leaders can do. Even if they're apostles! The apostles cannot manipulate the congregation into being generous. They cannot force them to care for widows as they would their own family. They can merely expect a lack of favoritism—and hope and pray for more.

Similarly, we must take care not to oversell our abilities as church leaders. It's rare that a complaint in my congregation comes my way that isn't in some way true. Is our congregation legalistic? I'm sure we are. Are we hard-hearted? I'm sure we are. Do we care too little about church planting? Quite certainly. Can I fix all this? No! I can pray that God would ignite real change; I can teach the congregation of God's priorities in his inspired Word; and I can address structural issues where they appear. But the problems that most pain us in our congregations are problems of the heart—and only God can do that work.

6. *Put our hope in what the Spirit can do through the congregation.* There's great news left for us in this passage, though! While church leaders have limited capacity for impact, God's Spirit can do amazing things. That's what we see at the end of the passage. Remember how the apostle's directive to choose *seven* men precluded equal balancing of Hellenists and Hebrews? Well, what did the congregation do? Most commentators I've read note that the names of the seven men of verse five are all Hellenistic.[6] In a congregation that was probably

---

[6] Of course, we can't say with certainty that *all* seven men were Hellenists. After all, Greek names were known among Hebraic Jews. But it would seem likely that at least a majority of these seven were Hellenists.

majority Hebrew, that's striking! Through a work of God's Spirit, the congregation didn't content themselves with simply meeting the bar the apostles had set for them; they bent over backwards to care for their Hellenist sisters. In a climate of mistrust and suspicion, they risked entrusting their widows to this unfamiliar cultural group. Why? So they could display the unity they shared in Christ. How this must have delighted the apostles! How this must have delighted God!

Not surprisingly, we read in verse 7 that "the word of God continued to increase," "the number of the disciples multiplied greatly in Jerusalem," and that "a great many of the priests became obedient to the faith."

So how should church leaders act when confronted with complaints and discontent? We should remember that threats to unity deserve our attention. That while leadership is our responsibility, it is ultimately the congregation who must address these threats. That we should generally avoid taking sides on the root cause of a problem—but seize opportunities to address structural problems when we see them. In doing so, we should have a realistic understanding of what church leaders can do, but unbridled optimism for what God's Spirit can do. And we should praise him when we see the truth of his gospel vindicated in our continued unity.

Playing the "Trust Me" Card

Putting this into practice will often lead to a dilemma, however. As church leaders, one of our greatest tools for protecting unity is to tell the church what to do and then ask them to trust us. After all, if everyone does as we say, there won't be any disunity, right? But, of course, that "trust me" card can be overplayed. And unless your church is substantially more mature than my own, you'll always raise some eyebrows when you simply say, "Trust me." Sometimes pastors say "trust me" too often, foolishly unaware that they've already overdrawn their trust account with the congregation. Other times they are too hesitant to reach for this tool, not realizing that they stand on a mountain of accumulated trust that should be spent for the unity of the church.

So when do we play this card? Here are some questions I hope will be helpful.

1. Is someone's reputation at risk? Let's say that many members of your congregation are upset that a certain man—we'll call him Jeff—is not an elder. Privately, you're aware that Jeff and his wife are struggling in their marriage. It would not be wise for him to serve right now, and beyond that, he does not meet the biblical requirement that he "manage his own household well" (1 Tim. 3:4). What do you do in a situation like this? Do you explain why Jeff is not serving as an elder? Of course not. Informing members of the church about the state of his marriage wouldn't help anyone. Instead, you winsomely explain why it is almost never appropriate to share why a man is not serving as an elder. But encourage the member to continue to bring names of men whom he or she thinks should be considered.

2. Does the concern pertain to a specific decision? Sometimes concern from the congregation has to do with a specific decision— such as ending the ability of nonmembers to volunteer in childcare. Other times, concern is more amorphous. For example, do people feel that the church is ignoring the needs of single adults? The "trust me" card is probably more appropriate in the case of a specific decision. In the case of the childcare policy decision, for example, the church leadership would be wise to lay out their reasoning to the congregation. They should encourage the congregation to ask questions. But ultimately, this is a good time for the congregation to trust the leaders God has given them. On the other hand, it would probably not be best for the leadership to simply say, "Singles aren't being ignored—trust us." How could that possibly be true in every situation? Instead of playing the "trust me" card, church leaders would do better to listen carefully. They should encourage those with concern to see what they can do as individuals about this perceived slight.

And they should consider any tangible, structural adjustments that might help singles.

3. To what degree do church leaders have better information than the congregation? Leaders—and especially church leaders—often have access to information that the rest of the congregation doesn't have. It could be information about a particular person's struggles, or a long history of caring for an individual, or financial details, or other information provided in confidence. When church leaders make a decision primarily in light of proprietary information, they should feel comfortable asking the congregation to trust them. This assumes, of course, that it is best for the information to remain private.

4. To what extent does the issue affect church unity? For example, one of the greatest challenges a congregation will ever undertake is excommunicating a member for being divisive (Titus 3:10). Divisiveness is inherently subjective. And often the goal of the divisive person is to divide the congregation from its leadership—who are the very ones charged in Titus with initiating this action. How do you determine that this offense has risen to the level of church discipline? Often, you're weighing the disunity that will result from divisiveness against the disunity that might result from playing the "trust me" card to excommunicate the offender. Play that card when it seems to be the best long-term strategy for protecting church unity.

5. How clear is the issue in Scripture? The clearer Scripture is, the less likely it is that you should play the "trust me" card. Let's say a dispute arises as to whether salvation requires repentance. Don't say, "Trust me"; show them what the Bible says! Reserve their trust in you for important issues that *aren't* clear in Scripture.

Some leaders err by playing the "trust me" card for nearly everything—failing Paul's requirement that elders be gentle and not quarrelsome (1 Tim. 3:3) and Peter's that they not be domineering (1 Pet. 5:3). Other leaders err by never asking for their congregation's trust, leading only where the sheep are already inclined to go. In that case, they ignore God's admonition to the congregation in Hebrews 13:17 that they "obey [their] leaders and submit to them." Surely God includes that command because sometimes a congregation should trust their leaders even though it's scary. May God give us all grace to learn when asking for their trust is the best way to serve our flocks!

Equipping Your People to Weather Discontentment

But now we should turn from defense to offense. So far, this chapter has focused on responding to difficult, unity-threatening situations—as the apostles did in Acts 6. But rather than simply waiting until a difficult situation arises, we want to prepare our people for these difficult times. As a guide, here are four topics that you should cover in your preaching, new members classes, and other teaching ministries.

1. The Importance of Unity

The idea that unity is good is not news. The problem is that we don't tell our people *why* it's good. Then, when unity seems to conflict with some other priority, our people don't know which to prioritize. When unity conflicts with gospel faithfulness, which should they choose? When unity conflicts with my preference for paint color, which should I choose? If we've never taught on why unity is important, how can we expect our people to make the right decision? After all, the reasons *we* value unity often diverge from the reason *God* values unity.

When you teach about church unity, denominate it in terms of its value to God. Yes, unity is pleasant. Yes, it makes for a happy church. Yes, it keeps meetings shorter. But ultimately unity is valuable because it reflects God's character and being (1 Cor. 1:13). More specifically, God cares about our unity because it shows off his power and wisdom.

2. Christians Act and Speak as Providers, Not as Consumers

Our churches must understand that Christians are spiritual providers, not consumers. The New Testament assumes that Christians ask, How can I serve? rather than What's in it for me? *All* Christians are to hold each other accountable (Matt. 18:15–20). *All* Christians are to encourage each other in faith (Heb. 10:23–25). And *all* Christians are to love deeply and sacrificially (Rom. 12:1–13). Spiritual consumers commit to a congregation to the extent that commitment benefits them; spiritual providers commit because of the benefit they've already received in Christ.

3. How to Publicly Disagree

We must teach our people when and how to publicly air disagreements with church leaders. Unless your church has no public meetings or online forums, I'm sure you've experienced the pain of public disagreement that should have stayed private. Or perhaps someone spoke in a church meeting who seemed frightfully oblivious to the impact his stridency could have on others.

Figure 8.1 teaches what our attitude toward public disagreement should look like in a church, depending on the issue.[7] Consider a particular disagreement someone might have with the church; for example, Should we teach the eternality of hell? Should we paint the bathroom gray or yellow? Then determine how clearly Scripture addresses the question and how important it is.

- *Clear and Important.* When the disagreement is in the upper right corner—both clear and important—getting to the right answer is more important than unity. Even at the cost of publicly breaking rank with church leadership and telling others to do the same, we must above all else be faithful to God's Word. Of course, defining *clear* and *important* is not without difficulty. By *clear,*

---

[7] You may have seen this same diagram used in other 9Marks publications to describe the various roles of elders, staff, and congregation in decision making.

I mean something that nearly everyone in a local congregation has historically seen as taught in Scripture. And by *important,* I mean an issue that is either essential to the gospel or essential to the preservation of the gospel. Note that by "public disagreement" I mean "disagree in front of the church." In almost no circumstance should a church dispute spill out into the world (1 Cor. 6:1).

- *Not Clear and/or Not Important.* Most disagreements will fall outside of this upper right quadrant. They may present good topics for spirited debates with church leaders in private, but they shouldn't spur an attempt to turn the congregation against its leaders. These are the "dissensions" and "divisions" that Paul holds up next to sexual immorality, sorcery, fits of anger, and orgies as works of the flesh characteristic of those who will not inherit the kingdom of God (Gal. 5:20–21). Even in private, members should not to waste their leaders' time with endless debates and "babble" (1 Tim. 6:20).

Fig. 8.1. Posture Toward Public Disagreement in the Local Church

	High	Unity is primary	Unity is secondary
Importance of the issue			
	Low	Unity is primary	Unity is primary
		Low	High

Clarity of the issue in Scripture

4. When to Leave a Church

We should teach our people when to leave a church. Sometimes, we act as if the job of church leaders is to "keep the peace" so that no one ever leaves. As if ours is the best possible church, and a parting of ways is always a failure. But in a fallen world, this stance is neither healthy nor realistic. The command of Hebrews 13:17 that we obey our church leaders is not simply instruction on what to do inside your church; it is also instruction on when to leave. If someone feels they can no longer trust their church's leaders, he should find a church where he can obey Hebrews 13:17. Especially as a church changes direction, it serves no one to only make changes that everyone agrees with. Just as Abraham parted amicably with Lot in order to preserve their friendship, sometimes the way a member loves his church is by leaving it.

I am quite certain that your church is not the best place for everyone. Some may find it too big; some too small. Some may find your leadership too autocratic; some too passive. Some may find your spiritual environment exhausting; some may find it bland. Use every departure as an opportunity to reexamine your ministry, but never assume that every departure is a mark of failure.

Your church's job is to shepherd every member to the greenest pastures, even when it means shepherding them into another faithful church. Of course, sometimes you suspect that the problem is the discontented person, not your church or your leadership. It would be tragic for such a people to run into exactly the same discontent in their new church. You may be able to show them this and encourage them to work through those issues in your church, where they're already known and loved. You may not. But in every situation, your job is to shepherd them to the best pastures they can find.

Conclusion

Protect the Flock

In his first letter, Peter instructs us: "Be sober-minded; be watchful. Your adversary the devil prowls around like a roaring lion, seeking someone to devour" (1 Pet. 5:8). Few areas pose as much risk to our churches as discontentment. What begins as a critique or a moment of insecurity turns sinful and tragic as members pursue selfish desires and sink into unhappiness and discord. Paul tells us in 1 Timothy 6:6 that "godliness with contentment is great gain." To promote this godliness, we must teach our congregations how to disagree well.

But quite often, what our congregations deal with isn't so much discontentment as it is sin. And sin in the church is yet another opportunity for the Devil to tear apart unity that should stand in praise to God's glory. How can we equip our congregations to protect unity when it's threatened by sin?

10

Addressing Sin in the Church

I'm sure you can recall examples of unchecked sin wreaking havoc on the community of your church. One person's sin starts small but eventually consumes the entire congregation—like the sin of Achan in Joshua 7. We need church members who take care to guard each other from sin. But growing a biblical culture in this area is not easy. Let me share two stories to illustrate.

What Kind of Church Culture Do You Have?

All Law, No Grace

"Burt" pastors a church plant in a thriving city. Unlike many church planters who build a fellowship out of nothing, he began with a core group of twenty families. Enthusiastic and committed, they had quit their jobs, said goodbye to their neighbors, and moved to an unfamiliar city to begin this new work. True to form, they take great care to root out sin in their midst. One-on-one or small group accountability is strongly encouraged, and the congregation shares honestly about its struggles. Men and women speak openly about struggles with pride, struggles in sexual purity, struggles with their money, struggles in their marriages . . . everything is on the table. But not all is well. People soon notice that their pastor exerts his authority in ways that seem intrusive. He'll tell you who to date, what car to buy, what job to take. And any hesitation at his "advice" meets with a quick reference to what must be his favorite verse: "Obey your leaders and submit to them" (Heb. 13:17). Many others in the congregation imitate his heavy-handed approach. They seem to value conformity more than sincerity. And beyond that, a sense of competition pervades the congregation, with members eager to claim credit for fruitful ministry under "their" purview. The church feels serious, zealous, and yet strangely cold—a feeling that only grows with time.

All Grace, No Law

Contrast that with a church pastored by "Chuck." God saved Chuck out of a lifestyle of breathtaking immorality. *Grace* is his favorite word. Years later, he still wonders that God should save him. During seminary, the moralism that others called "preaching" disgusted him; he determined to preach grace, grace, and more grace. So when he received his first pastorate, that's exactly what he did. Eschewing imperative verbs, he sees every command in Scripture as opportunity to marvel at Christ's perfect obedience and to drive us to the cross. And you can see that focus in his congregation. They are warm and welcoming people who speak often of God's love. But over time, you get the sense that while they discuss grace frequently, sin is quite private. A person may confess his own sin, but he'd never confront it in the life of another; that would be "legalistic." In fact, legalism seems to lurk in every shadow, and the congregation takes pains to avoid any scent of it. As a result, questionable decisions, foolishness, and even obvious sin go unnoted. Doesn't Jesus tell us not to judge lest we be judged?

"Balance" Is Not Our Goal

I don't know about you, but both of these churches can at times seem like my own.[1] Sometimes we seem intent on scrubbing the sin out

---

[1] These two stories are entirely hypothetical.

of each other's lives, as if sanctification were man's work and not God's. At other times, we meet any intrusive line of questioning with charges of "legalism," "judging," and "self-righteousness." But as is so often the case in the Christian life, the solution is *not* to simply chart the middle path between these two. We seek a church culture where it is normal for people to have deep and honest conversations about their spiritual lives. Where people are willing to ask that one last question that, while awkward, saves a brother from a difficult dynamic in his marriage. *And* where the gospel of grace is an everyday answer to struggle with sin.

This is not a "balance" between law and grace; it is a culture obsessed with serving others. An overzealous culture of legalism is rooted in self-righteousness. We show others their sin to prove our moral superiority. Similarly, a culture that backs away from difficult conversations about sin is rooted in self-preservation. We care more about peace than we do about holiness. In both cases, concern for "self" headlines our lives.

Contrast this with a church where Christ's reputation dominates our attention. There, we calibrate our conversations according to how we can best help others image Christ. There, we "speak the truth in love," varying our approach "as fits the occasion" with the ultimate goal of "giving grace to those who hear" (Eph. 4:15, 29).

Think for a moment about the culture of your own congregation. I'm not so much asking what you teach or what your church says it believes. I'm asking about the prevailing attitude of your congregation toward sin in their lives. Is yours a culture where people peg spiritual worthiness to relative holiness or fruitfulness? Is yours a culture that celebrates grace but where lives are shrouded in privacy? Or is it a culture that encourages honest, grace-filled conversations about sin and struggle? Given the rose-colored glasses through which church leaders often see their congregations, this might be a question better answered through conversation rather than introspection.

What if this culture is lacking? What can we do? In Matthew

18:15–17, Jesus gives us instructions about how to address sin inside the church. By considering his words carefully, we can go a long way toward fostering a culture that encourages honest, grace-filled conversation about sin. So for the rest of this chapter, we'll do just that. We'll start with Jesus's instructions about dealing with sin privately, then we'll look at his instructions on addressing sin publicly.

Equip Your People to Address Sin in Private

Like the other Synoptics, the Gospel of Mathew turns on Peter's confession of Jesus as the Christ. Much to Peter's surprise, however, are Jesus's next words: "From that time Jesus began to show his disciples that he must go to Jerusalem and suffer many things from the elders and chief priests and scribes, and be killed, and on the third day be raised" (Matt. 16:21). Jesus would one day come in victory to reign. But first he comes as suffering servant. Significantly, then, as soon as Jesus introduces this idea of a delay between his first and second comings, he also introduces the church. He establishes his church in chapter 16 (v. 18), distinguishes it from earthly government in chapter 17 (v. 26), and explains how it functions in chapter 18 (v. 15–20). Why? Because the church is his chosen vehicle to preserve his people until he comes again. Then, with this teaching on the church complete, Matthew turns the narrative in 19:1, to begin the road to the cross.

The reason I place these verses within the larger context of Matthew's Gospel is because we often underestimate them. We read Jesus's teaching on sin in Matthew 18 and see it as mere detail, something that is nice to know but relatively inconsequential in our lives. But when we look at it in the context of the whole book, we see the centrality of this teaching to Matthew's Gospel.

Now on to what Jesus says.

> If your brother sins against you, go and tell him his fault, between you and him alone. If he listens to you, you have gained your brother. But if he does not listen, take one or two others along with you, that every charge may be established by the evidence of

two or three witnesses. If he refuses to listen to them, tell it to the church. And if he refuses to listen even to the church, let him be to you as a Gentile and a tax collector. (Matt. 18:15–17)

In a fallen world, waves of sin will inevitably break over our churches. These verses offer crucial guidance for how our congregations should respond. How can we cultivate a culture of grace-filled honesty about each other's sin?

Recognize That Addressing Sin Is Our Responsibility

The first thing Jesus shows us is that we must address sin. *Ordinary church members* must address *each other's* sin. Notice that in verse 15 Jesus gives primary responsibility for addressing sin to each member of the congregation. It helps to pair this command with Jesus's earlier teaching in Matthew. If your brother sins against you (Matt. 18:15), you must seek to win him back. And if your brother perceives that you have sinned against him (Matt. 5:23), pursuing him is *still* your responsibility. No matter "who started it," it is always your job to initiate reconciliation. Add on top of this Paul's admonition in Galatians 6:1, "If anyone is caught in any transgression, you who are spiritual should restore him in a spirit of gentleness." Apparently, we have responsibility for rescuing each other from sin even when misdeeds are not directly against us.[2]

Turning a blind eye to sin is not an option. To be sure, there *are* situations where wrongdoing is so slight that love leaves it unaddressed (Prov. 19:11). And there *are* situations where lack of relationship or the right circumstances make it unproductive to approach a brother about sin. After all, the goal in Mathew 18 is to "gain" your brother, not merely to discharge your duty.[3]

---

[2] Paul's use of the word *spiritual* in Galatians 6:1 seems most likely to simply refer to those who, according to the previous verses, exhibit the fruit of the Spirit rather than the works of the flesh. Thus, in 5:25 he speaks of those who "live by the Spirit." In other words, he isn't designating some special group of mature believers who have responsibility for rescuing others from sin; he's saying that all believers share that responsibility.

[3] Consider Ephesians 4:29: "Let no corrupting talk come out of your mouths, but only such as is good for building up, as fits the occasion, that it may give grace to those who hear." Sometimes the occasion is not right for reproof.

But these caveats aside, we must teach our congregations their responsibility to love others by confronting sin. So when Joe comes to tell you about the hurtful thing Sally said to him, what's your first response? "Before you talk with me, have you talked with Sally about it?" With few exceptions, conversation about another's sin should either be confession (e.g., confessing my poor response when I was wronged) or collaboration (e.g., talking together about how we can encourage that person toward godliness).

And there's another side to this verse. We should make ourselves open to this correction. One virtue you can talk about, pray about, and teach about in your church is transparency. Our lives should be open to each other, and we should strive to be approachable when they're not. After all, if we hide our sin, how can any of us do what Jesus commands here? The Christian life is not one of posturing and preening; it is a life of honesty. Honesty about our money and marriages, our sins and struggles, our ambitions and anxieties. At least a few in your congregation should know pretty much everything about your life. The good news? Such transparency is contagious. Once some start taking risks to live this way, it will spread to others.

Following this portion of Jesus's instructions goes a long way toward fostering the kind of culture we desire. It battles against passivity as we embrace a God-given responsibility to rescue each other from sin and deception. And it protects against a self-righteous desire to speak about the sin of others instead of speaking to them.

Keep the Circle Small

Jesus is willing for an offense to go public if that's what it takes to win a brother's repentance (Matt. 18:17). But his instructions limit as much as possible the number of people who are aware of the sin in question. At first, the conversation is just you and your brother: "between you and him alone." If that fails, it is merely "one or two others" who accompany you to win the sinner over. With our own sin, we should be open and transparent; with the sin of others, we should be discrete. Yet how often do we stray from this principle? We talk openly about what a brother or sister has done—to vent, to seek pity, to rally friends to our side—instead of obeying Jesus and keeping the offense between the two of us.

In our efforts to foster church culture that is honest about sin without becoming self-righteous, this offers a good checkpoint. Self-promotion and self-righteousness want the circle of those who know of someone's sin to be as *wide* as possible. But when my goal is the exaltation of Christ through the restoration of a brother, I will keep the circle as small as possible for as long as possible.

As a pastor, I sometimes find people in my office seeking advice for how they should deal with the sin of others. And that's not necessarily wrong. But here are a few guiding questions that I ask them (or ask myself about them):

- Have you talked with the one who offended you? If not, why not?
- Is your goal in talking with me (as evidenced by your attitude) really to seek advice on how to love your brother or sister best? Or are you here to serve yourself?
- Are you trying to curry favor with me, push your God-given responsibility for confronting this person onto me, or show me how godly you are?
- Is the emotion you're feeling primarily one of compassion (because of how this brother is hurting himself and Christ through his sin) or offense and outrage (at how you've been treated)?

Be Slow to Judgment

Why does Jesus say to "take one or two others along with you"? Certainly one reason is the impression that this will make on the one caught in sin. But the specific reason Jesus gives alludes to the requirement in Deuteronomy 19:15 that conviction for a crime must be established by at least two witnesses. Jesus assumes that sometimes we are mistaken about a brother's sin—and that others will help sort out and clarify the facts. Having the humility to recognize the limitations of our own judgment can take a culture that's rightly serious about sin and fill it with grace as we give each other the benefit of the doubt.

The Goal Is to Gain Your Brother

"If he listens to you, you have gained your brother," says Matthew 8:15. This is our goal. Our goal is not merely to discharge a duty, or to get it off our chest. It is certainly not to punish; our goal is restorative. Yet here we must recognize the supernatural element of what Jesus describes. Only God can work heart change. Our job is merely to lift a mirror to a believer's heart so he can see his sin. We are reporters, not doctors.

Do you see how careful attention to Jesus's words helps to grow the kind of church culture we desire? Jesus gives us responsibility for guarding each other, so glossing over sin for the sake of peace is not an option. But at the same time, the goals he gives us are entirely at odds with self-protection and self-righteousness. What wonderful wisdom for us to follow in our teaching and example.

Seek Unity as You Address Sin Publicly

So far, we've worked through Jesus's instructions on dealing with sin privately. It's amazing how often our struggle with sin ends here. Despite our enemies of the world, the flesh, and the Devil; despite the unyielding deceitfulness of sin; despite our own corrupt nature—the grace of God at work in small, private conversations leads to repentance and restoration. But on occasion, we must read further in Matthew 18 because unrepentant sin has risen to a level that requires action by the church. Now that sin has gone public, the stakes are high. If we manage this conversation with the congregation well, it will do wonders for a culture of grace-filled honesty about sin. But if we manage it poorly, we will do untold damage. Here is what Jesus teaches: "If he refuses to listen to them, tell it to the church. And if he refuses to listen even to the church, let him be to you as a Gentile and a tax collector" (v. 17).

I do not intend to address in this short space the details of how to conduct church discipline. For that, I recommend Jonathan Leeman's short book, *Church Discipline*. For a more robust rooting of church discipline in the biblical idea of love, I recommend his volume titled *The Church and the Surprising Offense of God's Love*. Here, I have a much more focused ambition. I want to use Jesus's command in Matthew 18:17 to consider how we manage a public conversation about sin within the church.

"If He Refuses to Listen to Them, Tell It to the Church"

Sometimes we must tell the church about someone's sin.[4] When a person remains unrepentant through the first two steps of Matthew 18:15–16, when the sin is serious enough that we cannot overlook it, and when its existence is demonstrable, we must bring it to the church. Notice how Jesus circumvents some of the faulty ways we try to apply this. Ignoring such sin is not an option; his command is to "tell it to the church." Literally, to the "assembly." His instruction is not to "tell it to those who know the sinner" or "tell it to his small group" or "tell it to the elders." Rather, Jesus's concern is that we apprise the entire assembly of the situation. And consider that the first church was the church at Jerusalem—a congregation so large it initially had to assemble in the temple courts (Acts 2:41, 46).

Why is it important for the entire church to act, and not just those who know the sinner best? For one, it seems from the verses that follow this passage (18:18–20) that when a local church acts as a congregation, it bears a special authority before God. But beyond that, public confrontation of unrepentant sin is good for the church. Here's how:

---

[4] I don't intend to suggest that every church is sufficiently well-taught to engage in church discipline. In some situations, we face two equally unappealing options: not practicing church discipline when it is called for and proceeding with church discipline but destroying the church in the process. I think it is rare that the second of those two options is the more faithful of the two. For further reading on this, see Mark Dever, "'Don't Do It!' Why You Shouldn't Practice Church Discipline," *9MarksJournal* (November/December 2009), http://www.9marks.org/journal/dont-do-it-why-you-shouldnt-practice-church-discipline.

1. Making sin public underscores sin's seriousness and deceitfulness. I think of a recent situation where a man's ongoing struggle with pornography eventually gave way to more serious sexual sin that brought long-lasting consequences. When unrepentance finally forced that situation in front of the entire church, it had a sobering effect on the rest of the congregation. Men and women who struggled—privately—saw that hiding sin is like hiding a time bomb. In the weeks that followed, many talked about sin with their friends for the first time, exposing it to the withering forces of prayer, accountability, and love. By God's grace, the man in question repented as well and remains a member.

2. Making sin public underscores the possibility of repentance. One lie Satan feeds us about sin is that change is impossible. But when we deal with sin publicly, we consider passages like 1 Corinthians 5:5: "Deliver this man to Satan for the destruction of the flesh, *so that his spirit may be saved in the day of the Lord.*" It should be impossible to talk with your church about unrepentant sin without also talking about hope in real, God-given repentance and freedom.

3. Making sin public teaches your congregation how to address sin privately. Just as corporate prayer serves as "training wheels" to teach your congregation how to pray, church discipline guides your congregation through how to address sin. A biblically rooted, sober conversation as a church about unrepentant sin will provide a good model for your people.

Obey Jesus's command in Matthew 18:17 to address sin publicly, and you will affect dozens or even hundreds of private conversations—that together form your church culture.

"And If He Refuses to Listen Even to the Church . . ."

Sometimes we think of this entire verse as a single thought—as if "telling to the church" removes the person from fellowship. Normally, however, this is not the case.[5] Normally what Jesus describes happens in several stages. The church hears of the matter. The church speaks of its concern to the unrepentant sinner. That sinner has opportunity to listen. And then if he does not, the church removes him from fellowship.

In this step of Matthew 18, the church speaks with one voice to an unrepentant sinner. This kind of unity is critical for church discipline. When the church speaks in unity, it reminds us of our responsibility to guard one another from sin and deception. And when the church speaks in unity, it has power to stop a sinner in his tracks.

Yet church discipline is ripe with opportunities for *disunity*. Emotions run high, past friendships and loyalties cloud our perspective, leaders can appear severe, and the reasons for pursuing church discipline can get lost in the muddle. Church discipline requires unity—but it also threatens unity. How can church leaders strengthen unity through these difficult conversations? Here are a few suggestions:

Lead with clarity. You can imagine how difficult it is for a congregation to act with unity when the case for church discipline is unclear. Ideally, an issue should be quite clear before it comes to the congregation. Jesus never mentions elders in Matthew 18, but it is prudent for them to get involved before a matter comes to the church. Elders can serve the church well when they investigate, counsel, and deliberate until a matter of church discipline is pointed and clear. One good rule of thumb is to state to the congregation only facts that are objectively verifiable. If those facts alone don't make a clear case for church discipline, hold the issue back if at all possible until it becomes more clear.

Lean on Scripture. Nothing helps clarity like continually returning

---

[5] Sometimes—as for the situation in 1 Corinthians 5—a person's actions make his profession of faith so unbelievable that nothing the person could possibly say would convince the church of his repentance. In that case, "telling it to the church" happens simultaneously with the church taking action to excommunicate.

to Scripture. It is important to state the goals of church discipline from Scripture. And it is important to use biblical terms when discussing the sin at hand.

Look for trust. Church leaders should be unapologetic about asking their congregations to trust them. After all, the congregation isn't as familiar with a matter of church discipline as their elders, and they may not have access to important information that their elders should hold in confidence. Encouraging a congregation to give you their trust is often wise and loving. But there are times when, due to difficult circumstances or a congregation's maturity, a wise church leader will realize that asking for trust is a bridge too far. As an example, I remember a pastor who faced his first case of church discipline: a ninety-year-old church Sunday school teacher was acting divisively. Did he have good reason to excommunicate her? I believe so. Titus 3:10 makes it clear that divisiveness is grounds for church discipline. Excommunication would have been good for this church and for this woman. But would this have stretched this congregation's trust to the breaking point? I believe it would have. Cases of divisiveness are difficult for even a mature congregation to consider because they are inherently subjective. And a elderly woman well-known by the congregation is a very difficult first time to exercise church discipline. Wisely, this pastor saw how difficult it would be for his congregation to trust him and chose a different course of action. Our challenge is to determine when asking our flock to lean forward in trust will protect unity—and when for too many members that request will actually serve to fracture unity.

Labor for unity. Above all, we must labor for unity. Because the goal of church discipline is restorative rather than retributive, it's tempting to gear all of our actions and language toward winning back a lost sinner. But we must not forget our responsibility for the whole flock. As Paul charged the Ephesian elders, "Pay careful attention to yourselves and to *all* the flock, in which the Holy Spirit has made you overseers" (Acts 20:28). And, as Paul notes in the next verse, sometimes church members are actually "fierce wolves." In such cases our job shifts from protecting them to protecting the flock *from* them. Here's an example of a dilemma I've faced. A member's sin had led to a warrant for his arrest in a nearby jurisdiction. Do we tell the congregation about the warrant, which was highly embarrassing and would bring additional barriers to his being restored to the congregation? Unfortunately, absent that one fact, the case for excommunication was confusing. So as I presented the situation to the congregation, I focused more on what would protect their unity than what would protect this man's dignity—and I mentioned the arrest warrant. In general, we should prize congregational unity as more important than the good of the unrepentant sinner. Fortunately, it is rare that we can't work equally hard for both.

". . . Treat Him as a Gentile and a Tax Collector"

Finally, we reach the last phrase of Jesus's instructions to our churches. To excommunicate someone isn't to say that he is definitely not a Christian, nor that we can see into his heart (as only God can). Rather, it is a "no confidence" vote on his profession of faith based on the evidence of unrepentance. Thus, Jesus doesn't tell us to declare the person an outsider, or to judge the reality of his faith. He merely tells us to *treat* the person as an outsider. We do this, presumably, until we are able to welcome him back in with a credible profession of faith. Paul takes this up in more detail in 1 Corinthians 5. There, we are told we must judge the credibility of a person's claim to be "a brother" (vv. 11–13).

Clarity on exactly what we are doing in church discipline has significant benefits to the culture of grace-filled honesty that we seek in our churches. The nature of excommunication as described by Jesus is neither heavy-handed nor manipulative; it merely observes a discordance between profession and action. Neither is it insignificant: it effects a real change to our relationship with this person. And it does not presume what is happening in this person's heart. Instead, it judges what we can see in his life. All these are principles that you want to instill in your congregation's daily attitude toward each other's sin. By carefully explaining what church discipline is and what it is not, you will help them in this direction.

Conclusion
Amazed at Grace

D. Martyn Lloyd-Jones was one of the most influential preachers of the twentieth century, pastoring at Westminster Chapel in London from 1939 to 1968. I remember asking his daughter what the key to her father's long ministry was. And in typical, pointed clarity, she answered: "I don't think he ever got over his salvation. He never stopped being surprised by it."

That's what we want for our own congregations. Every day of their lives, we want them to stare in amazement at what God has chosen to do through the gospel. When they treasure salvation as undeserved grace, they will take seriously their responsibility to guard one another from sin. When they treasure salvation as undeserved grace, they will celebrate God's power to transform sin-ridden hearts. The more amazed we are at our salvation, the more we will foster a culture of honest, grace-filled conversation about sin.

But what exactly is the lasting fruit of biblical church community? Is it merely the good that God does *within* our churches? Or should that fruit extend beyond our congregations? That brings us to the final section of this book. We've studied how to nurture and protect a community that is evidently supernatural. Now we turn to the harvest that biblical community brings in evangelism and church planting.

Part 4

Community at Work

Evangelize as a Community

My friend Walter was an addict. Here's how *The Washington Post* told his story:

> He used crystal methamphetamine, and then he discovered crack cocaine. He was homeless for a time, and then he was a thief. He lived in doubt and fear, in paranoia and darkness, until one morning in 2010, when he went for a run.
>
> Barrera believes it was that experience, when he needed a break after only one block, that he replaced drugs with running. Three years later, its hold is as strong as any narcotic. Instead of waking each morning in search of the next high, he tried going a little farther than the previous day, a few more seconds without stopping. After a few weeks, he ran a 5K, and the feeling afterward was familiar.
>
> "Everything just feels perfect, feels right," he says.
>
> Soon he was running marathons, but eventually that wasn't enough. Barrera ran a 50-mile race last June, and three months from now—if the rain holds off often enough, if his legs stop sending pain through his body, and his old life spares his new one

of surprises, such as last year's jail term—he will run a 100-mile race in the mountains of Colorado.[1]

Reading the *Post* article, you would think that running saved Walter. And in one sense, it did save him—from homelessness, joblessness, and crack. But talk with Walter and he's quick to tell you that running merely changed the decor of his prison cell. True freedom came not from a run, but from a walk—through a train station.

Several months after Walter's first run, another friend of mine, Brady, walked through the train station looking for people to talk with about Jesus. He noticed Walter and passed him by. But his conscience was pricked, so he retraced his steps and asked if Walter wanted to talk. As Walter reflected later on, he'd noticed the Bible Brady was carrying and had an odd urge to ask him about it. But being the quiet type, he'd resisted. So when Brady walked directly up to him, he was surprised and delighted. They talked through the gospel, read through sections of the Bible, and parted company. Walter was intrigued, but still lost in his sin.

The next time they met, Brady started reading through the gospel of Mark with Walter. And he began introducing him to various members of his church, who introduced him to yet other Christian friends. One of those new friends sang a song on Easter Sunday about Christ's resurrection that Walter couldn't shake. At the end of a long run a few weeks later, with the lyrics of "Jesus Is Alive!" repeating through his head, Walter suddenly realized he believed Jesus *was* alive. On his knees, he trusted in Christ. By the time he was baptized, dozens in the church already knew his story.

So who led Walter to the Lord? Who gets to "notch his spiritual belt" with another miracle of conversion? Ultimately, it was the Lord himself, wasn't it? John 6:44 says, "No one can come to me unless the Father who sent me draws him." But whom did God use? Was it Brady, who had the courage to walk up to a stranger and explain the

---

[1] Kent Babb, "Walter Barrera's 12-Million Step Recovery Program," *The Washington Post*, May 24, 2013.

gospel? Was it Andy, who met him a few days later? Was it Mark, who preached one of the sermons God used to pierce Walter's heart? Or was it Shai, who sang that song?

I suppose you'd have to answer yes to all of these! In my experience, Walter's story is typical in the pattern it follows. For him, evangelism was *personal*. That is, he didn't simply wander into a church by himself, intrigued at what they had to offer. Instead, he first heard the gospel through a relationship with Brady, even if that relationship was only two minutes old. But evangelism wasn't merely personal—it was also *corporate*. It's difficult to pinpoint exactly who "led him to the Lord" since all sorts of people from the church were involved. "Mob evangelism" is how I like to describe it.

And the wonderful news about Walter is that this personal, corporate evangelism didn't stop with him. Shortly after his baptism, he told the church that before his conversion, he'd committed crimes that deserved jail time. Following Christ meant repenting of these things, so he turned himself into the authorities and went to prison to serve his sentence. While in jail, a congregation he hardly knew showered him with visits and letters. To his fellow prisoners, that love added weight and reality to the testimony of God's grace they heard from Walter. Before his release, Walter's cell mate also professed faith in Christ.

Evangelism Is Both Personal and Corporate

I love mob evangelism because it's so much more biblical than the evangelism we often practice. For one, I love it because it's personal. Rather than seeing evangelism as nothing more than inviting someone to church (and church as nothing more than a weekly evangelistic rally), mob evangelism shares the good news through relationships. It's how Paul shared the gospel: "We were ready to share with you not only the gospel of God but also our own selves, because you had become very dear to us" (1 Thess. 2:8). We should teach our churches that evangelism is something *they* do in their day-to-day lives, not something limited to our weekly gatherings or special church events. Evangelism should be personal.

But in addition to being personal, evangelism should be corporate. In our efforts to protect church from becoming an evangelistic rally, we should never think that evangelism has nothing to do with the church. After all, if the community of the local church is confirmation of the gospel message, we are fools to evangelize in isolation from it. Doing evangelism on my own is like digging a pit using a toy shovel, then leaning on a backhoe to rest. What magnificent power sits idle while I work! Why would you ever share the gospel with a friend without trying to expose her to the supernatural community of the local church? The witness of the local church is today's equivalent of what Paul describes in 1 Corinthians 2:3–5: "I was with you in weakness and in fear and much trembling, and my speech and my message were not in plausible words of wisdom, but in demonstration of the Spirit and of power, so that your faith might not rest in the wisdom of men but in the power of God." We want faith to rest in the power of God. And where else is God's power more visible than in the local church?

After all, this idea of the church community as evangelistic witness fills the Bible. Here's a brief tour.

- As early as Genesis 1, we begin to see God's plans to glorify himself through a *people* and not just individuals. God made male and female in his image, and then commanded them to "be fruitful and multiply and fill the earth and subdue it" (Gen. 1:28). In other words, they were to fill God's creation with living images of their Creator.

- More directly, when God creates his special people Israel, he tells them to show off his splendor to the nations through their life together. "Keep [my statutes] and do them, for that will be your wisdom and your understanding in the sight of the peoples, who, when they hear all these statutes, will say, 'Surely this great nation is a wise and understanding people.' For what great nation is there that has a god so near to it as the LORD our God is to us, whenever we call on him?" (Deut. 4:6–7).

- Accordingly, when God describes his rebellious people's failure, he cites this corporate mandate. Instead of showing the glory of his name, they had defamed his name among the nations (Ezek. 36:20–21).

- So as Jesus inaugurates a new people of God, he points again to the evangelistic witness of their life together in his new command: "By this all people will know that you are my disciples, if you have love for one another" (John 13:35). So often the way we talk about this verse, you'd think we forgot the words "one another" at the end. It's not just love that shows we are Jesus's followers—it's love for his other followers.

- As Luke introduces us to the church, then, in Acts 2, he describes their life together—how they broke bread together, devoted themselves to fellowship, and cared for each other's needs. "And the Lord added to their number day by day those who were being saved" (v. 47). Jesus's new command of John 13 was becoming reality.

- And in the New Testament Epistles, this remains a central theme. It is unity in the church that causes the heavens to stare (Eph. 3:10). It is love between brothers that evidences who are the children of God (1 John 3:10).

The local church is not evangelism. But the local church should be the power of evangelism. As such, evangelism should be both personal and corporate. It is personal; it generally involves explaining the gospel in the context of a friendship rather than simply bringing someone to church. And it is corporate; without introducing non-Christians to the local church, evangelism ignores the greatest evidence we have for the truth of the gospel.

Is Our Light Under a Basket?

As appealing as this sounds, though, it's not easy to put it into practice. How can relational evangelism expose unbelieving friends to the community of the local church in a postindustrial, postrural, post-Christian society? In a place where everyone in town knows everyone in town, the corporate witness of the church shines into all corners of society. To quote Jesus in Matthew 5:14–15: "A city set on a hill cannot be hidden. Nor do people light a lamp and put it under a basket, but on a stand, and it gives light to all in the house."

But what happens when half of the world's population—or in the developed world, nearly three-quarters—have fled to the anonymity of urban life? What happens when your average church member is driving twenty to thirty minutes to get to church, crossing three or four cities in the process? What happens when you are the only Christian your non-Christian friends know? In that world, how do we display the corporate witness of the church to a watching world? How do we get out from under this basket?

That's our topic for the rest of this chapter. We'll start with some ideas that you can put into place as a church member—and suggest to other church members. And then we'll turn to ideas you can put into place as a leader in your congregation. I pray these thoughts will help the corporate life of your congregation shine into the darkness of this fallen world.

Advice for Church Members

How can church members expose their non-Christian friends, coworkers, relatives, and neighbors to the attractive witness of our churches? Consider this list of ideas.

We Can Talk about Life in a Church

Honest transparency about life in a Christian congregation can go a long way toward this goal, even if a non-Christian friend doesn't have opportunity to meet others in your church. In other words, conversation about your faith shouldn't simply explain the gospel. It should also describe life in the church that the gospel produces. While we should avoid airing the church's dirty laundry to the world

(1 Corinthians 6), this doesn't mean we present a plastic, overidealized description of the Christian life. Just as you can talk about the vicissitudes of marriage while protecting the honor of your spouse, you can describe the glory and reality of life in a church in a way that brings praise to God. For example, I remember talking with parents at my son's bus stop about how our church was wrestling through the untimely death of a young mom. Or in my days in business before becoming a pastor, my Mormon colleague and I talked at length about my work as an elder (avoiding confidential information, of course). The Mormon ward he was assigned to was limited to single adults aged 31–45. So he was interested to hear about life in a church that was marked not by similarity but diversity.

We Can Mix Our Circles of Hospitality

Most Christmas mornings, the two retired men next door join our family for breakfast, along with a smattering of different people from church. Over the years, my two friends have heard the same message about the gospel and about our church from a wide variety of people. Along similar lines, I love how my friend Trevor uses his birthday party each year to expose Chinese graduate students in his apartment building to the community of his church. If you have non-Christian friends you've shared the gospel with, include some friends from church at meals with them. Invite them on a hike with your family and a few others from your congregation. Invite them to join flag football or a soccer match with a group from church on a Saturday. Recently, some coworkers of a church member came to a party he threw with a few others from church. Their reaction? Conversations seemed deeper and more real than what they normally experienced. So they decided to come on a Sunday morning to check this church out. I think we can easily underestimate the difference between the casual interactions of this world and the casual interactions of genuine Christians.

Invite Others to Join You in Evangelism

Let's say that another mom from your kids' school has begun to show an interest in the gospel. It indicates humility and love for her when you invite a few others from your church into the conversation. Perhaps over lunch you introduce her to your Christian friend Ana, and then quietly encourage Ana to study the gospel of John with this mom. Just as Brady let other people in on the joy of seeing Walter become a Christian, you do everyone a great service when you invite others into evangelistic conversations. If your church culture lauds those who singlehandedly "win" non-Christians to faith, set a better example. Pray that when God brings a friend of yours to Christ, your church community will have so embraced him that he wouldn't actually know *who* "won" him to faith.

Aspire to be a Neighborhood Church

For some readers, this piece of advice will fall flat simply because of where they live or the fact that their church doesn't have a fixed location. But many of us have opportunity to make church a geographic hub for our lives. And many who can't do this today will find it possible in the future. Just look at the portion of the population with driver's licenses (falling) or the value of homes in walkable communities (rising) or the prevalence of mixed-use development or the rise of retirement communities. All of these trends, at least in the United States, point to a population that is less geographically mobile and more neighborhood-centered than in recent decades. I think that this trend is one Christians should welcome and participate in. That web of acquaintances and friendships is powerful in its ability to shape perceptions, advertise commitment, and prompt real conversations about the gospel.

And if a neighborhood-centric mentality is unrealistic, consider locating your home near other church members, even if your church doesn't have a specific location. I think of several families from a church in Shanghai who have decided to live in the same high-rise apartment building. That puts their relationships on display to neighbors in a fast-paced city where so many feel displaced and unmoored from their roots.

Advice for Church Leaders

These ideas can apply to any member of any church. But for church leaders, I have some additional strategies to put your church's corporate witness on display to the watching world.

Aim Your Church Services at Christians

What is the main evangelistic value of your church service? Is it directly explaining the gospel to non-Christians? No. Church is for explaining the gospel to *Christians*, to fuel the supernatural witness of their community together. In 1 Corinthians 14, Paul makes it clear that the church assembles mainly to edify believers. Everything we do should aim at glorifying God by edifying each other.

As a church leader you are probably told frequently that if you would just make church less about Christians and more about non-Christians, you'd see more people saved. If you would just shorten your services, simplify your sermons, open up service opportunities to nonmembers, have classes that non-Christians enjoy, and so forth . . . you'd reach the lost for Christ. But if that were true, why does the New Testament devote so much of its content to how the local church can worship God by building up believers? When we begin to think about church gatherings as mainly opportunities for evangelism, we make a few mistakes.

- First, we forget that, absent supernatural community, the church can't compete with the world to attract non-Christians. For people bent on pleasure and ambition, the world will always be a more attractive place than your church to spend a Sunday morning. You can't out-world the world.
- Second, with many societies becoming increasingly post-Christian, people have lost any residual feeling that they *ought*

to go to church. That means that no matter how relevant you attempt to be to a non-Christian world, the main way non-Christians will come to you is through a relationship they already have with a Christian in your church.

- Most importantly, our greatest confirmation of the gospel is the community of the local church. Therefore, our best strategy for reaching the world is to fan that community into a raging inferno of supernatural witness that will be far more attractive than any adjustment to our music, small groups, or sermons could ever be.

How ironic that in the name of reaching the world, some churches have embraced a consumerist approach that only encourages self-oriented concern.

Make Church Services Accessible to Non-Christians

This might seem like odd counsel given my first point. But while Paul taught in 1 Corinthians 14 that our worship gatherings exist mainly for edification, he also had keen interest in the response of unbelievers to those gatherings (vv. 20–25). So preach sermons that address the unbelievers present. Observe ways in which the passage you're preaching undercuts common assumptions of the non-Christian world. Ask questions that beg for a Christian answer. Explain the gospel—not merely throughout the sermon, but in its entirety at some point in your address.

Similarly, explain what you're doing as you move through the service. And use transition points to explain your purpose for each element of the service.

Three important things happen when you make your services accessible to non-Christians.

First and most obviously, you help unbelieving attendees to engage with the service—even if they do so as outsiders. It's OK for them to feel like outsiders; just make sure they are welcomed and well-informed outsiders.

Second, you teach your church that it is normal for non-Christians to be present. They won't assume that everyone they meet after the service is a Christian simply because they are in church. And it will spur their thinking about including unbelieving friends at church.

Third, you teach your congregation how to engage with unbelief. You're showing them how to apply Scripture winsomely to the objections of a non-Christian. And you're showing all the ways in which the challenges of our world provide an on-ramp for the gospel.

Create a "Regulated Free Market" of Evangelistic Initiatives

Let's say that you're a pastor, and as you look at your church, your members aren't taking much initiative to do evangelism, let alone exposing the world outside to the community of the church. What do you do? We often see our options boiling down to one of two:

- *The programmatic approach.* In this option, you build corporate evangelism into the institutional life of the church. You organize regular evangelistic addresses at a local coffee shop, for example, or nursing home evangelism, or Wednesday night visitation in the neighborhood. You run these programs through your staff, fund them through your budget, and recruit for them from the church body. The problem with this approach, however, is that it can infantilize your members. It *tells* them how to live out the Christian life rather than encouraging Spirit-led initiative to live out Scripture. And beyond that, it does little to nurture a *culture* of evangelism; it merely feeds people into the programs you offer.
- *The organic approach.* In this option, you keep the institution of the church very simple; you focus on the Sunday gathering and little else. You preach the priority of evangelism and the power of communal witness—and then pray that your people will take initiative to live it out. But again, this approach has its problems. First, because people don't see evangelistic ministry highlighted publicly, they will often think it unimportant. And second, as a pastor, you certainly have some sense for which evangelistic

efforts will fare best; certainly, you want to point your flock in the right direction, don't you?

I think that a third approach would help. In this model, we lead with the preaching of the Word. Then as church leaders, we watch to see where that Word is taking root and flowering into action. And we respond by using church resources to support the most strategic of those ideas. Resources could include money in the church budget, co-ordination of volunteer resources through a weekly prayer meeting or online bulletin board, highlighting member initiatives in sermon application, or creating diaconal positions to facilitate various initiatives.

In this model, church leadership is reactive. We react to what our members choose to do. But we are not passive; we actively promote member-prompted ideas that deserve attention. Think of this as a regulated free market approach. On the one hand, it is a free market. Rather than *telling* people how to live out the Great Commission (as the programmed approach can do), we watch to see what naturally takes shape as the Spirit convicts through God's Word. Yet this is not wild, frontier capitalism. We deliberately help the best ideas to prosper, and unapologetically use the resources of the local church to do so.

Here's an example from my own experience. Years ago, several church members had an idea to start English classes on a nearby university campus, using the Bible to help students practice English. As this ministry grew, it became a great example of relational, corporate evangelism. The focus was building one-on-one mentoring relationships with international students that introduced them to the church community. As elders, we began talking about it more with the congregation. We used money from the church budget to support it. Then a funny thing happened. When students thought of the classes primarily as English lessons, their participation was minimal. But after a few years, word got around campus that the people teaching English were Christians who could also teach the Bible. At that point, participation grew to more than a hundred students, each with a church member as mentor. We created a diaconal position to coordinate all this effort. And we've seen more and more students putting their faith in Christ.

It's quite possible that over the next few years, interest in this initiative will wane and something else will prove more strategic for the gospel. If that's the case, our church leaders will reactively point people in a different direction. But, praise God, with each new initiative that bubbles up from God's work among the congregation, a culture takes root. It's a culture where evangelism is normal and evangelism as a community is normal.

In short, be patient and willing to let God's Word create initiative in your congregation. Then, as you see that initiative take root, reactively promote the best of it.

Train Your People to Evangelize—Together

Whenever I sit down with a Christian interested in joining my church, I ask them to share the gospel with me. I'm amazed at how many earnest Christians actually struggle to do that. Fortunately, many good gospel presentations and evangelistic training methods are available.[2]

Yet even in these excellent resources, something's often missing. These methods and tools rarely make any reference to evangelism as a corporate activity. So in your evangelism training, describe how evangelism functions in the context of the church. Highlight examples from the life of your church. Suggest additional ideas, like Christian neighbors jointly hosting an intro-to-Christianity study. Help them see how unfortunate it is to speak the message of the cross in isolation from cross-shaped community.

Conclusion
Aiming for a Deep Culture

In some churches, outreach is front-and-center, framed in bright lights. It's led from the front and heavily promoted. But often as you

---

[2] For a sampling, you can visit www.9marks.org/journal/evangelism-course-comparison-guide.

get to know these congregations, you find that there's not much happening beyond official church-sponsored activities.

Instead, we want a church where a passion for the lost is core to its personality. There may not be banners on the website, brochures in the lobby, or infomercials between songs on Sunday. But when you open up a church and poke around inside, you discover a whole world of evangelistic fervor. People share the gospel with friends, neighbors, and relatives. And, whenever possible, they're letting the congregation be both context and apologetic for evangelism. In a church like this, there may not be as much sheen on the surface, but the culture is deep. That's our goal.

But if we stop there, we haven't fully seen what biblical community can do in a local church. The local church isn't simply context and apologetic for evangelism. It is the goal of evangelism. Evangelism should result in new churches as we fulfill the Great Commission through church planting. How we bring biblical community to harvest through the birth of new churches is the topic of our next and last chapter.

12

Fracture Your Community

(for the Community of Heaven)

Church community is not an end in itself; it is to be a blessing to others. To draw an analogy from astrophysics, it is the ecclesiastical equivalent not of the all-consuming black hole but of the exploding quasar. It builds itself up, only to rocket its energy outward.

Chapter 11 looked at one way this happens, when community fuels evangelism. But evangelism alone stops short of our calling. When Jesus gave the Great Commission in Matthew 28, his followers didn't respond by simply sharing the good news. They planted churches. In fact, in Titus 1:5 we read that Paul considers his mission work in Crete unfinished until churches—with elders no less—are established. Your church community can bless others by giving birth to new community in other churches, both locally and globally. That's what this final chapter is about.

Making Yogurt

Think of this as the yogurt model of church planting. When you make yogurt, you can't just assemble raw ingredients and follow a recipe, because yogurt requires live and active cultures to grow. Instead, you'll need to start with some yogurt that's already made and add it to a container of warm milk. Then over a few hours the culture from the starter yogurt will grow, until you have a new batch to taste.

Quite often, we do church planting from a distance. We send money to fund a missionary to an unreached people group. Or we send a church planter off for training and then pray for him as he starts up a new congregation. But sometimes we have the chance to make some yogurt. We can take the live culture of our own congregation and see it grow into a new, healthy church community. Thus the name of this chapter: "Fracture Your Community (for the Community of Heaven)." Sometimes the most strategic thing we can do for God's kingdom is to take the precious fellowship he's raised up and split it apart. Then new churches can bear witness to the gospel far more effectively than we could ever do by ourselves. This may involve planting a church overseas. It may happen locally. Say a dozen families living in the same area go with an associate pastor and one or two elders to start a new church closer to their homes.

Why would we want to do this? Why is this "yogurt model" sometimes more attractive than simply sending money or a church planter? Quite simply, because nurturing church community is a long and difficult task. Think of all the decisions a new church must make about how it will function.

- What kind of leadership model do they see in Scripture?
- What level of theological agreement should be required for membership?
- What role will small groups play in pastoral care?
- When is divorce and remarriage allowed for in Scripture?
- How should worship services be structured?
- What role will mercy ministry play in the life of the church?

And so on.

In contrast, consider a healthy church community that already exists. There you'll find not just theological agreement, but agreement on what it looks like to "do church together." An existing church community will have a common perspective on so many potentially divisive issues. And more positively, they will share many assumptions about what it looks like to be a healthy church member. How wonderful to take that agreement into a church plant!

Now to be sure, there's nothing new about "hiving off" a portion of a congregation to create a new church. What may be new, however, is how the philosophy of church community in this book affects that idea. If community is something that can be manufactured at will, then you should plant churches as fast as humanly possible. Any church can plant at any time simply by cutting itself in two. After all, you can quickly rebuild this kind of community. Yet the church community I've described isn't something we can manufacture; it's something we cultivate, as God makes it grow. So we need to think less like a factory worker and more like the viticulturist, expanding a vineyard by judiciously cutting and grafting a living vine. An understanding of how church community grows and thrives should inform our approach to church planting.

Is Your Church Community Ready to Replicate?

You must begin with the basic question of whether your church is ready to plant. Pastors often talk of having church planting "in the DNA" of their churches. Great objective. But we must ask whether the rest of the DNA is also worth replicating. Is your church community sufficiently formed as to be a blessing if it is reconstituted into a new church? Consider the answer to these questions about your own flock:

1. Is your congregation clear on the gospel? If you were to ask random members of your congregation what the good news of the cross is, how would they answer your question? There's no reason even a congregation full of new believers shouldn't be able to do this well. But in many of our churches, we're not there.

2. Is your congregation telling others the gospel? Church planting is the natural result of evangelism, and it won't work well without it.

3. Do your church members teach God's Word to each other? Is yours a church culture where it's normal to encourage each other with Scripture?

4. Does your congregation take their responsibility seriously to guard each other from sin? Are those conversations both honest and grace-exalting?

5. Is most of the pastoring in your church done by the congregation? Is it unusual for a pastoral problem to come to your attention where ordinary members of the congregation are not already at work?

6. Do you already see a breadth and depth of relationships that cannot be explained by natural bonds alone? Have these types of relationships come to characterize your congregation?

7. Does your congregation trust its leadership? Or is it still typical that disunity erupts when leaders make a challenging decision?

If your congregation can't answer "yes" or "by and large" to these seven questions, I fear your church's DNA is not yet worth replicating. You may be involved in the Great Commission financially, by supporting church planting locally and among unreached peoples around the world. You may even raise up church planters to do good work elsewhere. After all, even unhealthy churches can produce great pastors and missionaries. But as a congregation, you will need to mature further before your community is ready to birth a new congregation. By slowing down now, you will likely bear much more fruit over the lifetime of your church.

Yet I haven't set a particularly high bar for the maturity needed to replicate a congregation, have I? I hope that most people reading this book will be able to say, "Yes, God *has* created church community that is supernaturally attractive"; "Yes, our church *is* at the point where we have DNA worth replicating." For you, another challenge remains, which will consume the remainder of this chapter. Since

God has built something wonderful into your congregation, how do you harvest it for the purpose of church planting? I'll answer in three parts.

Think beyond Planting

First, I want you to consider something beyond church planting. Perhaps you live in an area like mine where church buildings dot the landscape. By God's grace, some of these churches faithfully preach the gospel. But many of them don't. With those that don't, think about them like synagogues in the first century for Paul. They are God-fearers who are lost. And even worse, they think they're fine, even though they're not. They've been lying about Jesus for decades by telling the community around them that Jesus is like a gossip, a slanderer, a back-biter, and an adulterer, when he's not any of those things. Some of us should try to help these churches. In fact, these reforming situations are especially well-suited to the yogurt model of church planting. Unlike church planting from scratch where no church culture exists, church revitalization replaces an unhealthy church culture with one that is more biblical. With that as your goal, you'll find that the culture that a portion of your congregation brings with them will be an important asset. If you're in the position to "make yogurt," I'd strongly encourage you toward the unique and strategic opportunity you have to revitalize an existing congregation and not just plant a new one.

What does this look like? Certainly not like a church takeover. You want to make known in your area that you're willing to send money, a pastor, and people to help a dying congregation get a new start. You want to be clear that your intention is not to simply make that church into a copy of your own, but to give it some fresh DNA and see it grow in its own context. Here are a few guidelines should you ever have the opportunity to do this:

1. Consider revitalization only when you can guarantee good preaching. Remember that supernatural community begins with

supernatural faith, which comes from hearing God's Word. You'll need solid preaching if you hope to see spiritual resurrection.

2. Send some of your elders. The first time my church tried something like this, we sent a gifted pastor and a dozen faithful members to a small, dying church. Things worked out well—but the loud feedback we heard was that this pastor needed elders with him.[1] Since then, we've never attempted a revitalization unless some of our elders (and men close to being recognized as elders) decided they wanted to go as well.

3. Clarify that you don't want to control the new church. Little can hamper your ability to help other churches more than the impression that you're merely an empire builder. Your job is to help—not to take over—these churches. So when you send people over, make it clear that their new church should be the main recipient of their giving, since that's where they now get their main teaching (Gal. 6:6). Structure the arrangement so that your church has no veto power over decisions of the new church. And so forth.

4. Cooperate freely. Just because this new church isn't part of your corporate structure doesn't mean you can't do things together. Freely offer advice as they seek it. Give money to get them off the ground. Offer them access to your administrative staff and your counseling ministry. Help them with bookkeeping and facilities management. Invite them to participate in your missions trips. There's no reason they need to replicate every function of your church—at least not at first.

A Pace That's Sustainable

Now for a second consideration. Whether you plant or revitalize, you'll need to watch the strain you're placing on the mother church community. In a church based on low commitment ministry-by-similarity—which this book has argued against—that strain

---

[1] You can read about this experience in Mike McKinley, *Church Planting Is for Wimps* (Wheaton, IL: Crossway, 2010).

might not be noticed. A relatively shallow level of community is quickly rebuilt. But if your church aspires to the type of community you've read about in the preceding pages, transplanting those old growth trees to a new church will seriously affect your own church community.

Sometimes that consideration is beside the point. An opportunity for a new church is so strategic and appealing, your congregation will want to seize it no matter the cost. But generally, you should balance your church's need for old growth with the opportunity to foster healthy church community elsewhere. Here are some ideas for how you can monitor the health of your community so that church planting doesn't stretch you too far, too fast.

1. Periodically review various elements of your church culture with your elders. How is your culture of discipling? Your culture of evangelism? Is the congregation caring well for each other? Do people seem accustomed to having honest, spiritually oriented conversations?
2. Ask questions during new-member interviews about how the church feels. We all know that church culture is more caught than taught; conversations with new members are an ideal way to gauge how well that's going.
3. Assess the quality of elder candidates. Are promising candidates leaving so quickly for various church plants that you have few men to consider for that important office? Or do you still have a few men who might begin serving as elders in the coming years?
4. Monitor the median tenure of your eldership and membership. Church planting will often shift your membership and leadership toward those who are newer. But sharp shifts in median tenure might be an argument to slow down, because long-term members are generally more critical to the fabric of a church community. Or if that number is going up, you might want to push the congregation to plant more quickly.
5. Consider the quality of your church leaders. Generally, if leaders leave with a new plant and others step up to take their place, that

is good for everyone's spiritual growth. But if you feel you are functioning without a sufficient number of mature leaders, you may need to slow down.

6. Recognize your own bias. Are you the conservative type who never quite feels ready to lose a section of your congregation? Or is "too fast" not in your vocabulary? Talk about your bias with the rest of your elders and let them compensate for you.

Pastor Those Who Go

Finally, you'll need to help the members of your congregation decide if they'll stay or leave. If you've endeavored to build biblical community in your church, this decision will be challenging for many. Your people should consider where they live, where they could live, what types of relationships they have in your church, how easy it is to build relationships, how well they're doing spiritually, and so much more. Pastor them through these decisions. As a starting point, here are ten questions I've found useful to ask my own church members when they consider leaving our church to join a new gospel work elsewhere.

1. Why are you considering leaving with the plant or revitalization? In these circumstances, you should leave for positive reasons— not to escape something about your church or because you feel guilty for staying.

2. Do you agree with the philosophy of ministry and theology of the church you're going to?

3. Is the new church one you can bring your non-Christian friends to?

4. How are you doing spiritually? If you're growing quickly, you should probably stay where you are. Don't stop a good thing! If you're not doing well spiritually, you should probably stay as well and let your current church help you. If you're doing fine spiritually—but are not unusually attached to your existing church— you're a good candidate to leave with a new work.

5. Is the new church a better fit with your situation? Smaller size, needs you can meet, or proximity to a ministry opportunity that excites you can all be good motivators to leave with a church plant or revitalization.

6. What kind of ministry do you have in your current church? Be careful before you leave when a particular ministry depends on you. On the other hand, if you're not a "net exporter" of ministry at present—in evangelizing, discipling, and encouraging—there's little reason to think that a new church would change that. Often the best candidates for leaving a church are those who are fruitful—and who envision themselves being even more fruitful somewhere else.

7. Is there a particular church planter you want to support? What an encouragement you might be if you uprooted your job, your family, and your home to follow a pastor or missionary to a new gospel work.

8. Do you live near your church? The further you live from your church, the more likely it is that moving to a church closer to home will better serve God's kingdom.

9. What state are your church relationships in? If you leave a church to avoid dealing with broken relationships, you'll likely bump into those same problems after a few years at your new church.

10. What do you want? How is God shaping your desires? We have freedom in Christ, and there is often more than one good choice in front of us. Praise God for that freedom!

Conclusion
Blessed in Order to Bless

Many books advocate an outward-focused church. Many books advocate rich church community. But many in the "outward-facing" crowd seem to ignore the transformative power of a community that is evidently supernatural. Too often, they view church as nothing more than a means to evangelism and church planting. And the "rich community" crowd often gets it wrong too. When warm, nurturing,

therapeutically beneficial church community becomes an end in itself, it obscures the fact that the church's most essential purpose lies
outside of itself.

To that unfortunate tradeoff, the opening words of Psalm 67 offer
refreshing correction.

> May God be gracious to us and bless us
>   and make his face to shine upon us, *Selah*
> that your way may be known on earth,
>   your saving power among all nations.

Why ask God to bless us? Why invoke Aaron's blessing that God
would "make his face shine upon us"? For our own comfort, our own
satisfaction, or our own glory? No: "that your way may be known on
earth, your saving power among all nations." Pray that God would
bless us, that community in our churches would be evidently supernatural. And pray that in evangelism and church planting, this community would bear fruit far beyond our own churches.

Conclusion

What's the difference between reading The Lord of the Rings and watching Peter Jackson's film adaptation? If you're a purist, you'll note quickly that the movies don't do justice to Tolkien's masterful prose. True enough. But the books don't quite take the place of the movies either, do they? No matter how well you know the books, the movies are mesmerizing. We would never tell someone *only* to read the books or *only* to watch the movies. There is a strong partnership between what you read and what you see.

A similar partnership between God's Word and church community is precisely what was recovered in the Protestant Reformation. Working from passages like Matthew 16:17–19, where Jesus establishes the church and gives it the keys of the kingdom of heaven, the Reformers described two "marks of a true church." One was the right preaching of the Word, the other was the right practice of the sacraments. And for the Protestant, the sacraments mark out the community of the local church. Through baptism, we enter that community; the Lord's Supper verifies that we continue in it. As a friend of mine put it, baptism is akin to our Christian birth certificate; the Lord's Supper is our passport. To be sure, God's Word is the source of all life for a church. But when defining the local church, the Reformers described a partnership between the right preaching of the Word—what we hear—and the right practice of the sacraments—the community we see.

I've written this book because I fear that too many have forgotten the importance of seeing. On the one hand, some churches have become too attraction-focused. They do anything to draw a crowd so that once people come they can hear the gospel. But a desire for people to hear has resulted in a tepid community that is not worth seeing. On the other hand, some churches believe that because they preach the Word correctly, they have done all that matters. Perhaps through legalistic or conformist impulses, their community has lost the vibrancy we see in Scripture. Again, the glory of what we hear is incongruous with the embarrassment of what we see.

I've written this book for church leaders who trust the perfection of God's Word. I've written it to help them unfold the Word they hear into a community they can see—so that "all people will know that you are my disciples, if you have love for one another." With this lens in place, let's review the book in brief:

- Chapter 1 taught us that not all community is created equal. Some churches have only gospel-plus community, derived entirely from natural means. But our aspiration should be gospel-revealing community that displays the power of the Word we hear through the community that we see.

- Chapter 2 examined what happens to the hearing of God's Word if what people see in our churches isn't evidently supernatural. We compromise evangelism, since church community is perhaps our greatest testimony to the truth of the gospel. And we compromise discipleship, since God's normal means of preserving our faith is a community we can see that reinforces the Word that we hear.

- Chapter 3 studied a depth of commitment that undergirds church community. Community built entirely on Comfort-Based Commitment looks little different from the surrounding world. But Calling-Based Commitment (church membership) fosters relationships with depth beyond what is natural. And that's something we can see.

- Chapter 4 discussed breadth in a church community. Ministry by similarity may create a kind of community, but when we look at it, we see something that differs little from the world outside. Yet true belief in God's Word naturally generates a diversity of community that is remarkable to behold.

- Chapter 5 focused in on the interplay between what we hear and what we see. Right preaching of God's Word aims to foster the right community of God's people.

- Chapter 6 was about prayer. How can we pray together for God's Spirit to do the unseen work that results in community worth seeing?

- Chapter 7 laid out a practical framework for cultivating a church of spiritually intentional relationships. In that paradigm, the bulk of "ministry" in a congregation is the thousands of small conversations and actions springing from God's Word that form the rich community we seek.

- Chapter 8 assessed structural impediments to biblical community in a church. How can our design of staff positions, events, music, and ministries facilitate or hamper breadth and depth of community?

- Chapter 9 examined how the apostles addressed discontent and disunity in the Jerusalem church. When disagreement strikes, unity between God's people should be the visible effect of God's Word.

- Chapter 10 walked through Jesus's teaching about sin in the church. When we are careful to follow his instructions, we create a culture of honesty and grace that can be experienced and seen—and that testifies to the transformative work of the gospel.

- Chapter 11 spoke of community as evangelistic witness. When God has created something truly supernatural in your church, how can you expose it to non-Christians so that the fruit God's Word has borne becomes something they can see?

- Chapter 12 examined how biblical church community comes to harvest through church planting and revitalization. This is perhaps the most important way that the Word we hear results in something we can see.

When Faith Becomes Sight

But, of course, we must remember that this community is quite temporary. Church community isn't meant to last; it merely foreshadows the community we will experience forever. Sometimes when my church is celebrating the Lord's Supper, I let my gaze drift from person to person, imagining what they will be like in heaven. There's Margaret over there who sends me all those discouraging e-mails—yet who loves her Lord and our church. Squinting into the future, I can almost see her now, shining with the wise love and compassion of her Lord. Joe, who's sitting a few rows back, reliably tells it as he sees it. That may at times be off-putting today, but the beauty of the honesty underneath will one day result in heartfelt praise to our King. Then there's Marie, who's talked with me a dozen times about struggles with unbelief. I can picture her gazing with unending joy and confidence on her faithful Redeemer.

"Him we proclaim," wrote the apostle Paul, "warning everyone and teaching everyone with all wisdom, that we may present everyone mature in Christ" (Col. 1:28). We also toil to that end, with eyes half focused on the glorious yet broken congregations in front of us—eyes half focused on the beauty of what they are becoming. As Mr. Spurgeon put it:

> I am occupied in my small way, as Mr. Great-heart was employed in Bunyan's day. I do not compare myself with that champion, but I am in the same line of business. I am engaged in personally-conducted tours to Heaven; and I have with me, at the present time, dear Old Father Honest: I am glad he is still alive and active. And there is Christiana, and there are her children. It is my business, as best I can, to kill dragons, and cut off giants' heads, and lead on the timid and trembling. I am often afraid of losing some of the weaklings. I have the heart-ache for them; but, by God's grace, and your kind and generous help in looking after one another, I hope we shall all travel safely to the river's edge. Oh, how many have I had to part with there! I have stood on the brink, and

I have heard them singing in the midst of the stream, and I have almost seen the shining ones lead them up the hill, and through the gates, into the Celestial City.[1]

May we love the community God has given us in our churches. May we love who they are, who they are becoming, and what God intends to do through them. May we hold onto them in love until they too have passed through those gates, and into their everlasting reward.

---

[1] C. H. Spurgeon, *Autobiography,* vol. 2 (London: Passmore and Alabaster, 1898), 131. No modern reprint with this quotation is yet available.

General Index

Scripture Index

9Marks

Building Healthy Churches

9Marks exists to equip church leaders with a biblical vision and practical resources for displaying God's glory to the nations through healthy churches.

To that end, we want to see churches characterized by these nine marks of health:

1   Expositional Preaching
2   Biblical Theology
3   A Biblical Understanding of the Gospel
4   A Biblical Understanding of Conversion
5   A Biblical Understanding of Evangelism
6   Biblical Church Membership
7   Biblical Church Discipline
8   Biblical Discipleship
9   Biblical Church Leadership

Find all our Crossway titles
and other resources at
www.9Marks.org